Content

MW01678642

About WE

WE is a movement that brings people together, and gives them the tools to change the world. Our unique family of organizations empowers people at home, around the world, and with our social enterprise. With **WE Charity**, we empower domestic and international change; with **ME to WE**, we create socially conscious products and experiences.

Get involved as a family

You can join the WE Movement as a family—bonding together and building lasting memories as you rally around causes that matter to you. WE provides the inspiration, resources, and support you need to take action as a family, helping you raise caring and compassionate children. There are many ways you can participate in the WE movement, and make giving back a part of your family life. Your family can learn more about the lives of youth in developing communities, raise awareness or funds for social issues, volunteer in your community or on a life-changing trip overseas—and so much more!

Get involved at school

Live WE at school by getting involved as a class volunteering, fundraising, or raising awareness around causes that matter. We can all make a positive impact! The WE Schools program provides education resources and service campaigns, helping students further their curricular learning and develop the life skills for success. WE Schools resources are free to schools and are always evolving to keep the learning materials fresh and relevant. For teachers, it revitalizes their class, the curriculum, and everyone's passion.

Join the Movement

Being empowered to change the world is what the WE Movement is all about. Taking the pledge on WE.org is where it all begins. Join us. We can't change the world without you.

IN SUPPORT OF

WE

The WE Pledge

I pledge to live WE by making a difference every day. We know that change starts with each of us and that together, we will change the world.

Craig and Marc Kielburger

Humanitarians, activists and social entrepreneurs, brothers Craig and Marc Kielburger believe that together, WE can change the world. Over 20 years ago, they set out on a bold mission: to work with developing communities to free children and their families from poverty and exploitation. Their vision expanded to include empowering youth at home, connecting them with global issues and social causes, and partnering with schools to inspire young change-makers from within the classroom. And with the launch of ME to WE, they created an innovative social enterprise that provides products that make an impact, empowering people to change the world with their everyday consumer choices.

Counting by 5s and 25s

Count by 5s.

1.	0, **5**, ____, ____, ____, ____, ____
2.	155, ____, ____, ____, ____, ____, ____
3.	730, ____, ____, ____, ____, ____, ____

Count back by 5s.

4.	275, ____, ____, **260**, ____, ____, ____
5.	860, ____, ____, ____, ____, ____, ____
6.	1000, ____, ____, ____, ____, ____, ____

Count by 25s.

7.	250, **275**, ____, ____, ____, ____, ____
8.	200, ____, ____, ____, ____, ____, ____

Count back by 25s.

9.	625, **600**, ____, ____, ____, ____, ____

Counting by 10s

Count by 10s.

1.	20, ______, ______, ______, **60**, ______, ______
2.	133, ______, ______, ______, ______, ______, ______
3.	224, ______, ______, ______, ______, ______, ______
4.	486, ______, ______, ______, ______, ______, ______
5.	3452, ______, ______, ______, ______, ______, ______

Count back by 10s.

6.	100, ______, ______, ______, ______, ______, ______
7.	891, ______, ______, ______, ______, ______, ______
8.	3240, ______, ______, ______, ______, ______, ______

BRAIN STRETCH

A box has 100 snack bars. Write how many snack bars are in

a) 2 boxes ______ **b)** 3 boxes ______ **c)** 5 boxes ______ **d)** 7 boxes ______

Counting by 100s and 1000s

Count by 100s.

1.	100, **200**, ______, ______, ______, ______, ______
2.	220, ______, ______, ______, ______, ______, ______
3.	315, ______, ______, ______, ______, ______, ______
4.	127, ______, ______, ______, ______, ______, ______
5.	302, ______, ______, ______, ______, ______, ______

Count by 1000s.

6.	1000, ______, ______, ______, ______, ______, ______
7.	2150, ______, ______, ______, ______, ______, ______
8.	3249, ______, ______, ______, ______, ______, ______
9.	2009, ______, ______, ______, ______, ______, ______
10.	3652, ______, ______, ______, ______, ______, ______

Growing Number Patterns

In a growing pattern, the number increases.

	+6		+6		+6		+6		+6		+6	
6		12		18		24		30		36		42

The pattern rule is add 6 each time.

1. Continue growing the pattern by adding.

a) The pattern rule is add 9 each time.

0, ______, ______, ______, ______, ______, ______, ______

b) The pattern rule is add 7 each time.

7, ______, ______, ______, ______, ______, ______, ______

2. What number was added to the pattern?

a) 20, 26, 32, 38 Add ______ each time.

3. Write the rule for the pattern.

a) 1, 9, 17, 25, 33 ________________________________

Shrinking Number Patterns

In a shrinking pattern, the number decreases.

	−10		−10		−10		−10		−10		−10	
90		80		70		60		50		40		30

The pattern rule is subtract 10 each time.

1. Continue the shrinking pattern by subtracting.

a) The pattern rule is subtract 3 each time.

30, _______, _______, _______, _______, _______, _______, _______

b) The pattern rule is subtract 5 each time.

45, _______, _______, _______, _______, _______, _______, _______

2. What number was subtracted to make the pattern?

a) 40, 36, 32, 28 Subtract _____ each time.

b) 140, 132, 124, 116 Subtract _____ each time.

3. Write the rule for each pattern.

a) 41, 34, 27, 20 ______________________________________

b) 300, 294, 288, 282 __________________________________

Extending Patterns

To extend a pattern, find the difference between each set of terms. Then write the rule.

1, 4, 6, 9, 11, … Rule: Start at 1. Add 3, then add 2.

Extend the pattern using the rule: 1, 4, 6, 9, 11, 14, **16**, **19**,…

1. Find the difference between each set of terms. Write the rule. Then extend the pattern.

+3 ___ ___ ___

a) 32, 35, 39, 42, 46, ______, ______, ______,

Rule: ____________________________________

___ ___ ___ ___

b) 74, 79, 81, 86, 88, ______, ______, ______,

Rule: ____________________________________

___ ___ ___ ___

c) 40, 38, 35, 33, 30, ______, ______, ______,

Rule: ____________________________________

___ ___ ___ ___

d) 65, 55, 50, 40, 35, ______, ______, ______,

Rule: ____________________________________

Extending Patterns (continued)

2. Create a growing pattern. Write the rule, then extend the pattern. Trade patterns with a classmate and solve.

3. Start at 1 and multiply each term by 3 to get the next term. Write the first four terms of the pattern.

4. Omar has 80 health bars. He eats 4 every day on a hiking trip. How many does he have left after 6 days? Write a pattern to show your work.

80, ______________________________

BRAIN STRETCH

Look at the pattern: 7, 11, 16, 20, 25, ...
Whose pattern rule is correct? What errors did the others make?

Brian
Start at 7 and add 4 each time.

Mason
Add 4 each time.

Julie
Start at 7, add 4, then add 5.

Using a Table of Values

Sally makes a growing pattern with beads.
The T-table shows the number of beads each time.

Figure 1 Figure 2 Figure 3

The pattern rule is start at 3 and add 3 each time.

Figure	Number of Beads
1	3
2	6
3	9

1. How many beads are added each time? Write the rule. Then continue the pattern.

a)

Figure	Number of Beads
1	2
2	4
3	6
4	

Rule: ______________________

b)

Figure	Number of Beads
1	1
2	6
3	11
4	

Rule: ______________________

c)

Figure	Number of Beads
1	3
2	8
3	13
4	

Rule: ______________________

d)

Figure	Number of Beads
1	3
2	9
3	15
4	

Rule: ______________________

Using a Table of Values (continued)

2. Complete the table of values. Write the pattern rule.
How many dots will Figure 5 have?

a) Rule: ___________________________________

Figure 1

Figure 2

Figure 3

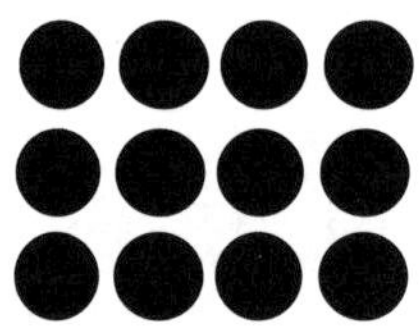
Figure 4

Figure	Number of Dots
1	3

Figure 5 will have ______ dots.

b) Rule: ___________________________________

Figure 1

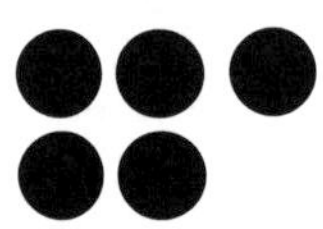
Figure 2

Figure 3

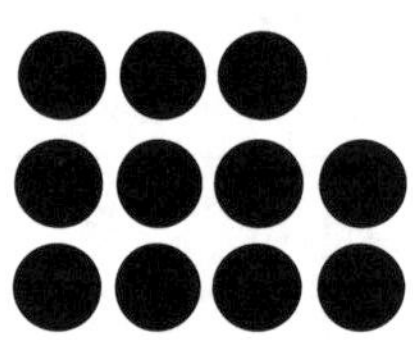
Figure 4

Figure	Number of Dots

Figure 5 will have ______ dots.

Comparing and Ordering Numbers

1. Count by 100s. Fill in the missing numbers.

Just before: **710**, 810, 910	Just before: ____, 300, 400
Just after: 1200, 1300, ____	Just before and after: ____, 3300, ____
Between: 589, ____, 789	Just after: 230, 330, ____

2. Circle the larger number. Hint: Read the numbers in each pair starting from the left. Underline the first digits that are different in each pair.

a) 439
469

b) 594
583

c) 2248
2294

d) 3411
2389

e) 537
527

f) 1435
1456

g) 954
959

h) 2111
2122

3. Order each pair of numbers from smallest to largest.

a) 435 345 ________

b) 549 538 ________

c) 2348 2349 ________

d) 3421 2399 ________

e) 5421 5423 ________

f) 6210 6110 ________

g) 899 989 ________

h) 432 342 ________

Comparing and Ordering Numbers (continued)

4. Order each group of numbers from largest to smallest.

a) 95, 84, 123 ________, ________, ________

b) 245, 212, 289 ________, ________, ________

c) 2546, 3254, 2134 ________, ________, ________

d) 4259, 5278, 5189 ________, ________, ________

e) 324, 234, 435, 543 ________, ________, ________, ________

f) 1456, 1532, 1879, 1346 ________, ________, ________, ________

5. Write 1000 more than or 1000 less than.

a) 2000 is ____________ 3000

b) 4500 is ____________ 3500

c) 10 000 is ____________ 11 000

d) 23 500 is ____________ 24 500

Comparing and Ordering Numbers (continued)

6. Compare numbers using < or >.

a) 4298 ____ 4199

b) 9239 ____ 9299

c) 10 567 ____ 10 657

d) 12 298 ____ 11 289

e) 23 458 ____ 24 267

f) 43 320 ____ 42 230

7. Make the greatest three-digit number using each set of digits. Use each digit only once.

a) 3, 5, 8 ______________

b) 5, 4, 9 ______________

8. Make the smallest four-digit number using each set of digits. Use each digit only once.

a) 4, 3, 7, 2 ______________

b) 5, 8, 3, 1 ______________

Thousands, Hundreds, Tens, and Ones

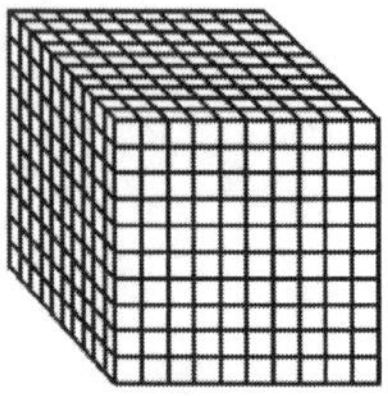 = 1000 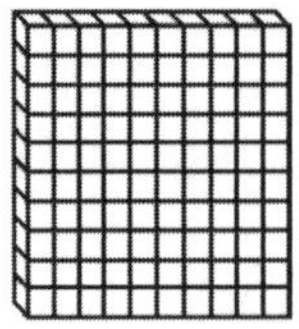 = 100 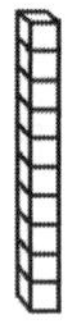 = 10  = 1

1 thousand + 1 hundred + 1 ten + 1 one = 1111

Count the thousands, hundreds, tens, and ones. Write how many blocks in all.

1.

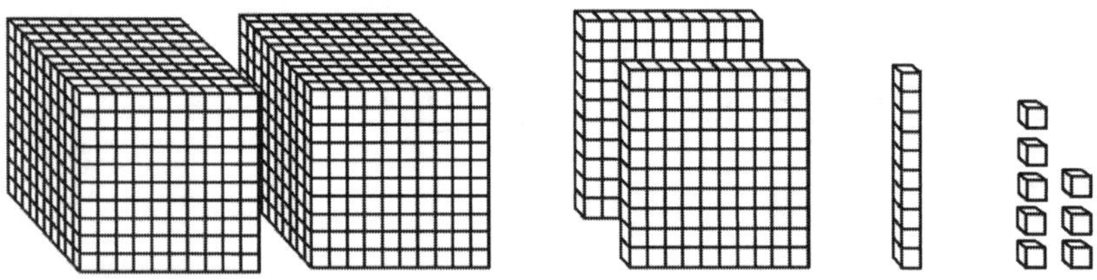

___ thousands + ___ hundreds + ___ tens + ___ ones Number _____

2.

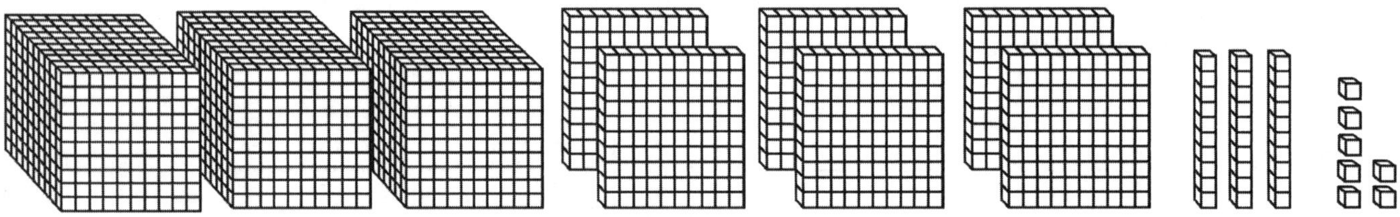

___ thousands + ___ hundreds + ___ tens + ___ ones Number _____

3.

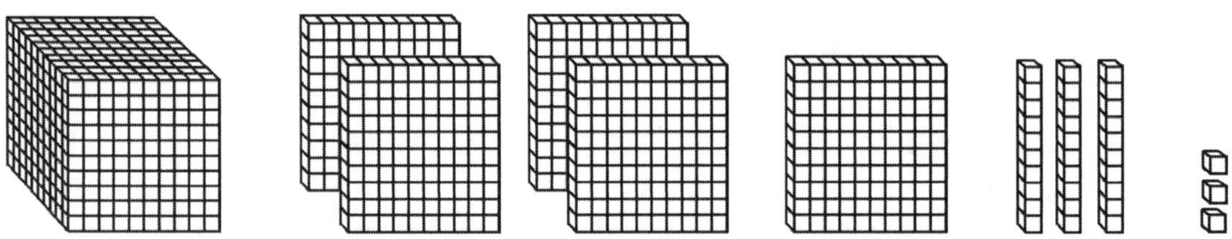

___ thousands + ___ hundreds + ___ tens + ___ ones Number _____

Thousands, Hundreds, Tens, and Ones (continued)

Count the thousands, hundreds, tens, and ones. Write how many blocks in all.

4. 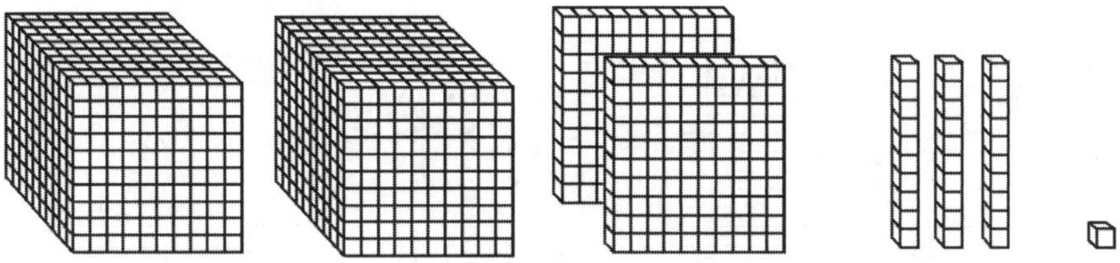

___ thousands + ___ hundreds + ___ tens + ___ ones Number ____

5. 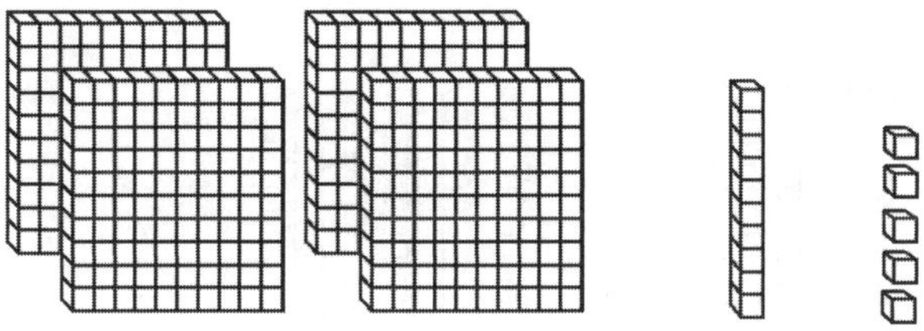

___ thousands + ___ hundreds + ___ tens + ___ ones Number ____

6. 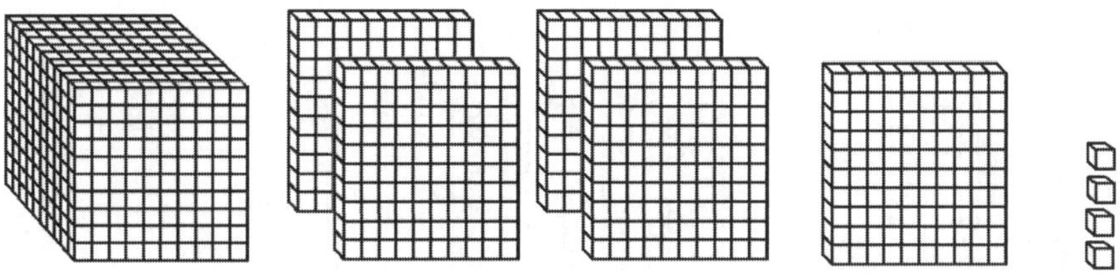

___ thousands + ___ hundreds + ___ tens + ___ ones Number ____

BRAIN STRETCH

Draw base ten blocks to show 1234.

Thousands, Hundreds, Tens, and Ones (continued)

Count the thousands, hundreds, tens, and ones. Write how many blocks in all.

7.

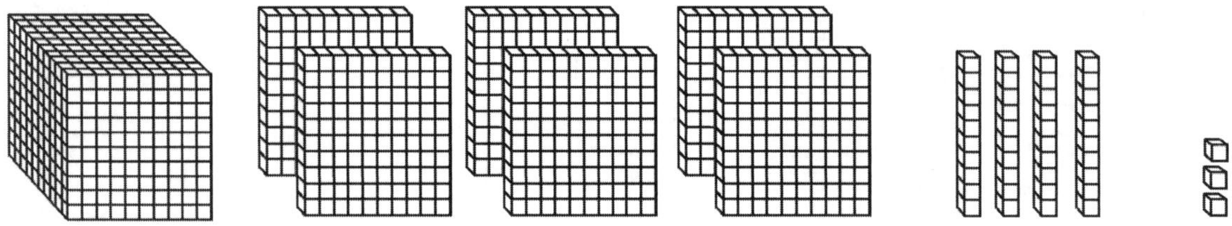

___ thousands + ___ hundreds + ___ tens + ___ ones   Number ____

8.

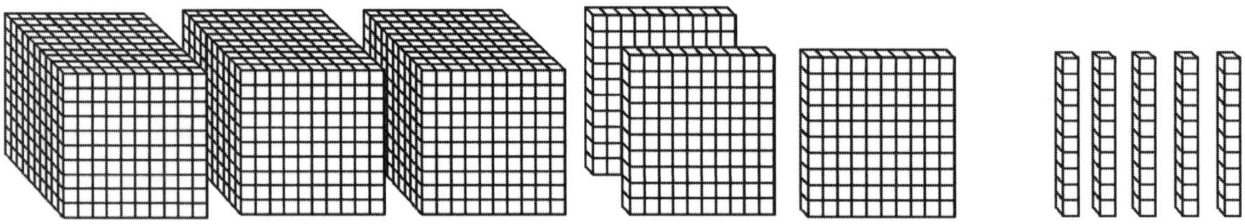

___ thousands + ___ hundreds + ___ tens + ___ ones   Number ____

9.

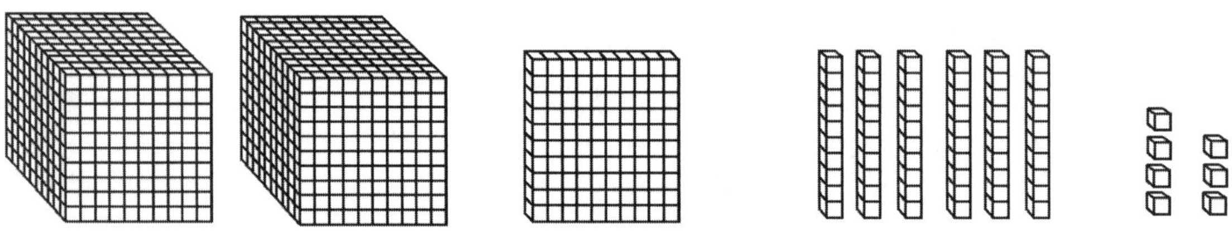

___ thousands + ___ hundreds + ___ tens + ___ ones   Number ____

10.

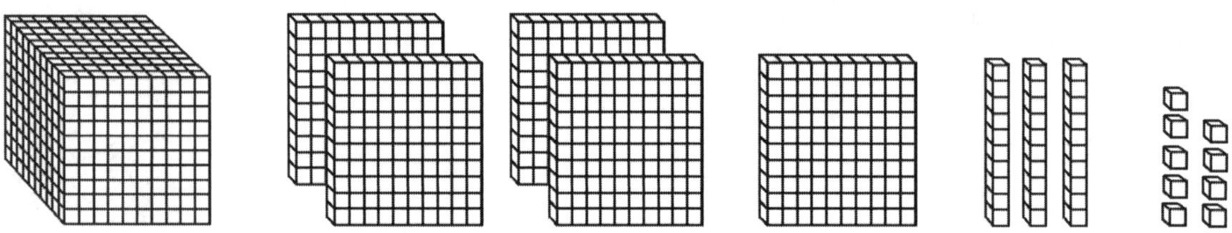

___ thousands + ___ hundreds + ___ tens + ___ ones   Number ____

Explore Place Value

For the number 3726
3 stands for 3000
7 stands for 700
2 stands for 20
6 stands for 6

Place value chart

thousands	hundreds	tens	ones
3	7	2	6

3726 in expanded form is **3000 + 700 + 20 + 6**

1. Write the place value of the underlined digit.

a) 565 **500**

b) 3721 ____________

c) 5260 ____________

d) 4622 ____________

e) 3428 ____________

f) 4527 ____________

2. Write each number in the place value chart.

	thousands	hundreds	tens	ones
a) 2347				
b) 4596				
c) 9875				

3. Write each number in expanded form.

3476 ____________ 6258 ____________

4. Write the value of each digit in the number 10 345.

____

What's the Value?

1. Write the missing value.

a) 2000 + 500 + 20 + _____ = 2529

b) 1 thousand + _____ hundreds + 2 tens + 4 ones = 1324

c) ______ + 600 + 80 + 1 = 7681

d) 4 thousands + _____ hundreds + 0 tens + 4 ones = 4704

e) _____ + 600 + _____ + 7 = 3647

2. What is the value of the digit 4 in each number?

a) 3489 _______ **b)** 4235 _______

c) 1254 _______ **d)** 3549 _______

BRAIN STRETCH

Compare and write >, <, or =.

a) 1804 ______ 1728 **b)** 2430 ______ 3375

c) 6664 ______ 6668 **d)** 7891 ______ 7891

Writing Numbers in Different Ways

Circle two correct ways to make each number.

1. 1141	**1140** + **1**	**1** thousand and **1** hundred and **4** tens and **1** one	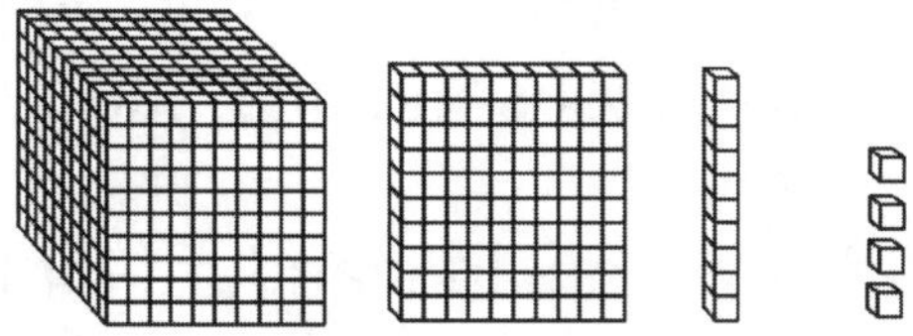
2. 1229	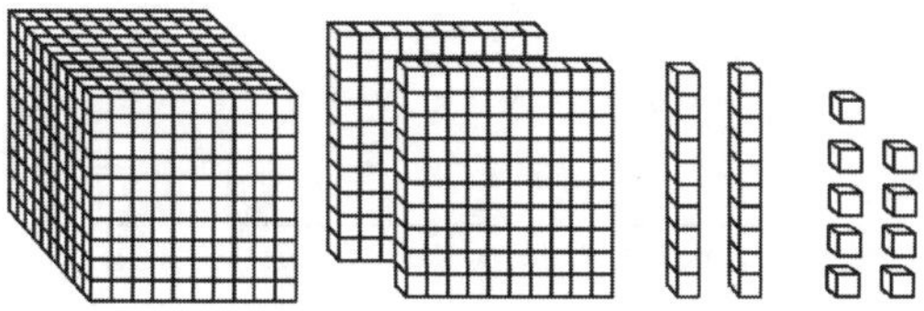	**1** thousands and **2** hundreds and **2** tens and **9** ones	**1000 + 200** + **2** + **9**
3. 1316	**1** thousand and **3** hundreds and **1** ten and **6** ones	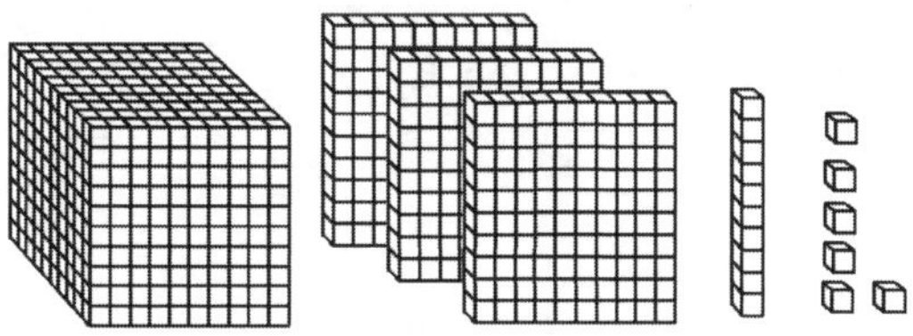	**1000 + 10** + **6**
4. 2153	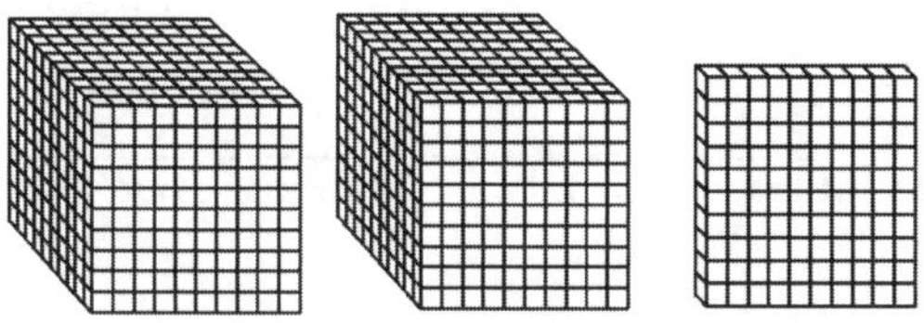	**2** thousands and **1** hundred and **5** tens and **3** ones	**2000 + 100** + **50** + **3**
5. 3290	**3** thousands and **2** hundreds and **9** tens and **0** ones	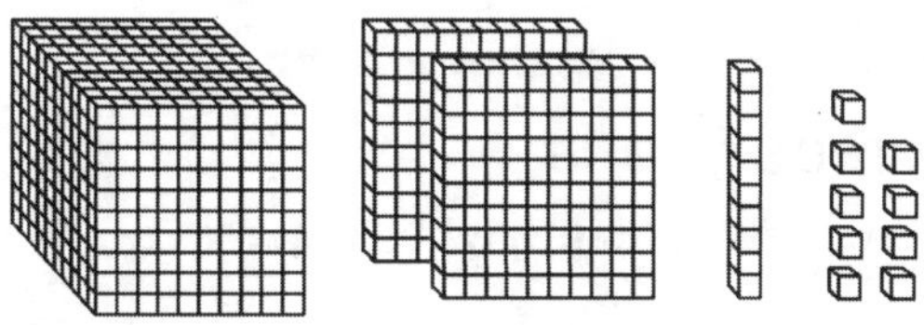	**3000 + 200** + **90** + **0**
6. 6365	**6** thousands and **3** hundreds and **6** tens and **5** ones	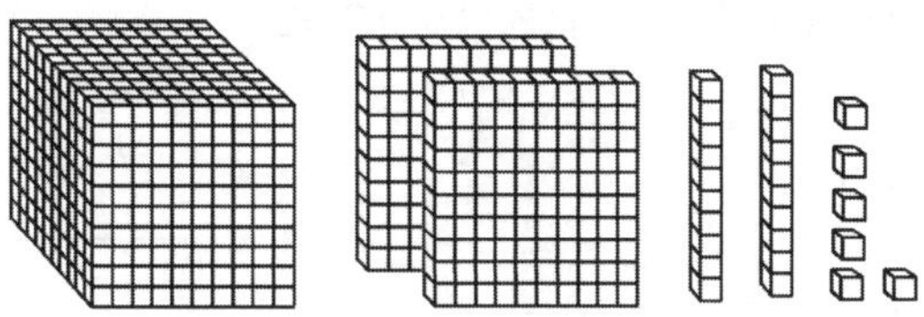	**6000 + 300** + **60** + **5**

Writing Numbers in Standard Form

There are different ways to write a number.

2000 + 100 + 10 + 7

2 thousand + 1 hundred + 1 ten + 7 ones

two thousand one hundred seventeen

2117

2117 is written in standard form.

Write each number in standard form.

1.	200 + 40 + 8	______
2.	3 thousands	______
3.	four thousand three hundred ninety-two	______
4.	7000 + 200 + 60 + 3	______
5.	1 thousand 3 hundreds 2 ones	______
6.	eight thousand two hundred thirteen	______
7.	9000 + 800 + 50 + 6	______
8.	two thousand one hundred eighty-nine	______
9.	4 thousands 6 hundreds 5 tens	______
10.	forty-five	______
11.	6 thousands 4 hundreds 3 tens 9 ones	______
12.	2000 + 500 + 80 + 1	______

Writing Number Words

Number words for the teens: eleven twelve thirteen fourteen fifteen sixteen seventeen eighteen nineteen

Number words for the tens: twenty thirty forty fifty sixty seventy eighty ninety

The number word for
3285 is three thousand two hundred eighty-five
12 345 is twelve thousand three hundred forty-five
220 123 is two hundred twenty thousand one hundred twenty-three

1. Write the number word.

a) 2121 **two thousand one hundred twenty-one**

b) 1234 ______________________________

c) 2465 ______________________________

d) 1390 ______________________________

e) 12 125 ______________________________

f) 50 237 ______________________________

2. Write the number word.

a) There are ______________________ days in a year.
365

b) Some months of the year have ______________ days.
30

Other months have ______________ days.
31

c) There are ______________________ seconds in a minute.
60

d) There are ______________________ seconds in one hour.
3600

e) There are ______________________ seconds in one day.
86 400

Number Round Up

To round to the nearest ten, look at the ones digit.

For 345, underline the ones digit. The 5 means to round up.
Round 345 to 350.

To round to the nearest hundred, look at the tens digit.
For 2347, underline the tens digit. The 4 means to round down.
Round 2347 to 2300.

To round to the nearest thousand, look at the hundreds digit.
For 3627, underline the hundreds digit. The 6 means to round up.
Round 3627 to 4000.

0, 1, 2, 3, 4
Round down.

5, 6, 7, 8, 9
Round up.

Round each number.

	Number	Round to nearest 10	Round to nearest 100	Round to nearest 1000
1.	8931			
2.	1103			
3.	7939			
4.	6902			
5.	4653			
6.	8727			
7.	5594			
8.	6738			
9.	5077			
10.	6043			

Estimating Sums and Differences

Estimate by rounding

to the nearest ten	to the nearest hundred	to the nearest thousand
63 → 60	389 → 400	1426 → 1000
+ 48 → + 50	+ 234 → + 200	+ 1644 → + 2000
110	600	3000
63 + 28 ≈ 110	389 + 234 ≈ 600	1426 + 1644 ≈ 3000

≈ means "approximately equal to"

1. Estimate by rounding to the nearest ten. Then add or subtract.

Example:

35 + 17

≈ **40** + **20**

= 60

a) 15 + 19

≈ ___ + ___

= _____

b) 41 + 34

≈ ___ + ___

= _____

c) 51 – 18

≈ ___ – ___

= _____

d) 76 – 23

≈ ___ – ___

= _____

2. Estimate by rounding to the nearest hundred. Then add or subtract.

a) 235 + 179

≈ ______ + ______

= ______

b) 378 – 113

≈ ______ – ______

= ______

c) 457 + 378

≈ ______ + ______

= ______

3. Estimate by rounding to the nearest thousand. Then add or subtract.

a) 2335 + 1700

≈ ______ + ______

= ______

b) 4389 – 2345

≈ ______ – ______

= ______

c) 3560 – 1110

≈ ______ – ______

= ______

Add by Making an Easier Problem

65 + 29 =

I know 29 + **1** = **30**.
I can add **30** to 65 to get **95**.
Then I subtract **1** to get **94**.
65 + 29 = **94**

1. Make an easier problem using tens. Then add.

a) 44 + 18 =

I know 18 + ____ = ____.

I add ____ to **44** to get ____.

Then I subtract ____ to get ____.

44 + 18 = ____

b) 53 + 27 =

c) 77 + 16 =

d) 36 + 35 =

e) 63 + 28 =

f) 48 + 39 =

Add by Making an Easier Problem (continued)

2. Use tens to help you add. Show your work.

a) 46 + 18 = ______

b) 59 + 16 = ______

c) 37 + 43 = ______

d) 68 + 29 = ______

e) 26 + 35 = ______

f) 16 + 67 = ______

g) 23 + 58 = ______

h) 71 + 26 = ______

Three-Digit Addition Without Regrouping

Line up the ones, tens, and hundreds.

Add the ones.

hundreds	tens	ones
2	2	3
+ 3	4	5
		8

Next add the tens.

hundreds	tens	ones
2	2	3
+ 3	4	5
	6	8

Then add the hundreds.

hundreds	tens	ones
2	2	3
+ 3	4	5
5	6	8

1. Use a hundreds, tens, and ones chart to help add. Shade the ones column yellow. Shade the tens column orange. Shade the hundreds column green.

654 + 235	162 + 115	370 + 127	115 + 761	644 + 110
418 + 530	386 + 512	572 + 223	484 + 301	943 + 16
152 + 803	231 + 606	453 + 321	751 + 137	314 + 530
462 + 335	612 + 325	330 + 414	270 + 113	156 + 503

Three-Digit Addition Without Regrouping (continued)

2. Use the hundreds, tens, and ones chart to add. Shade the ones column yellow. Shade the tens column orange. Shade the hundreds column green.

153 + 14 = ____	755 + 131 = ____	233 + 504 = ____	154 + 523 = ____	171 + 315 = ____
324 + 53 = ____	323 + 224 = ____	474 + 111 = ____	437 + 222 = ____	426 + 132 = ____
235 + 553 = ____	452 + 127 = ____	163 + 714 = ____	234 + 612 = ____	541 + 312 = ____
441 + 333 = ____	216 + 261 = ____	583 + 412 = ____	513 + 236 = ____	611 + 255 = ____
303 + 446 = ____	315 + 634 = ____	734 + 211 = ____	815 + 154 = ____	885 + 113 = ____

Three-Digit Addition with Regrouping

Line up the ones, tens, and hundreds.
Add the ones.
Then add the tens.

If there are more than 9 tens,
trade 10 tens for 1 hundred.
Regroup in the hundreds column.
Write the tens.
Add the hundreds.

hundreds	tens	ones
1		
3	3	6
+ 2	9	3
6	2	9

Trade 10 tens from 120 for 1 hundred.
Regroup by writing 1 in the hundreds column.

1. Use a hundreds, tens, and ones chart to help add. Shade the ones column yellow. Shade the tens column orange. Shade the hundreds column green.

564 + 375	322 + 492	176 + 472	538 + 290	143 + 173
312 + 194	387 + 441	594 + 270	421 + 380	656 + 183
664 + 175	334 + 282	124 + 393	162 + 383	430 + 392

Three-Digit Addition with Regrouping (continued)

2. Use the hundreds, tens, and ones chart to add. Hint: If there are more than 9 ones, trade 10 ones for 1 ten. Regroup in the tens column.

□ 1	□ □	□ □	□ □	□ □
239	377	565	658	625
+ 412	+ 219	+ 216	+ 124	+ 119
651				

□ □	□ □	□ □	□ □	□ □
335	924	343	627	148
+ 338	+ 27	+ 219	+ 164	+ 538

□ □	□ □	□ □	□ □	□ □
457	729	844	249	555
+ 419	+ 148	+ 18	+ 441	+ 327

3. Add. Regroup where necessary.

1 1	□ □	□ □	□ □	□ □
379	289	457	585	679
+ 23	+ 138	+ 177	+ 257	+ 135
402				

Four-Digit Addition with Regrouping

Line up the ones, tens, hundreds, and thousands.
Add the ones. Add the tens.

If there are more than 9 hundreds,
trade 10 hundreds for 1 thousand.
Regroup in the thousands column.
Add the hundreds and then the thousands.

thousands	hundreds	tens	ones
1			
3	9	0	6
+ 3	2	9	3
7	1	9	9

Trade 10 hundreds from 1100 for 1 thousand.
Regroup by writing 1 in the thousands column.

1. Add by regrouping where needed. Use a place value chart to help you. Shade the ones column yellow, the tens column orange, the hundreds column green, and the thousands column blue.

3464 + 1355	2202 + 7488	6575 + 3372	5269 + 1820	4364 + 2933

4212 + 5138	5379 + 3411	3904 + 2361	1429 + 2180	3636 + 2173

Hint: Regroup in more than one column.

2754 + 4375	4335 + 3578	6125 + 1938	5268 + 3923	3417 + 4992

Subtract by Making an Easier Problem

44 – 18 =

I know 18 + **2** = 20.
I can subtract **20** from 44 to get **24**.
Then I add **2** to get **26**.
44 – 18 = **26**

1. Make an easier problem using tens. Then subtract.

a) 34 – 29 =

I know 29 + _____= _____.

I subtract _____ from **34**

to get _____. Then I add _____to get _____.

34 – 29 = _____

b) 54 – 27 =

c) 67 – 38 =

d) 71 – 26 =

e) 81 – 38 =

f) 92 – 47 =

Subtract by Making an Easier Problem (continued)

2. Use tens to help you subtract. Show your work.

a) 46 – 17 =

b) 55 – 16 =

c) 37 – 18 =

d) 68 – 29 =

e) 56 – 27 =

f) 75 – 47 =

g) 65 – 39 =

h) 82 – 55 =

Add and Subtract by Making an Easier Problem

38 + 5 = 38 + 2 + 3
= 40 + 3
= 43

53 – 39 = 53 + **7** – **32**
= 60 – 32 Think: 60 – 30 – 2
= 28

1. Use tens to help you add. Show your work on another piece of paper.

a) 46 + 18 = ____ **b)** 59 + 16 = ____

c) 37 + 43 = ____ **d)** 68 + 29 = ____

e) 26 + 35 = ____ **f)** 16 + 67 = ____

2. Use tens to help you subtract. Show your work on another piece of paper.

a) 46 – 13 = ____ **b)** 55 – 16 = ____

c) 37 – 18 = ____ **d)** 68 – 29 = ____

e) 56 – 27 = ____ **f)** 75 – 47 = ____

3. Use tens to help you add and subtract.

146 + 26 = ____

I know 26 + 4 = 30

146 + 30 = 176

176 – 4 = 172

a) 259 + 18 = ____ **b)** 537 + 29 = ____

c) 466 – 48 = ____ **d)** 664 – 35 =____

Taking Apart to Make Tens for Subtraction

> 31 – 6 = 31 + **<u>4</u>** – 6 + **<u>4</u>** = 35 – 10 = 25
> 6 + 4 = 10 So, add 4 to each number.

1. Make an easier problem using 10. Then subtract.

a) 15 – 9 = 15 + **<u>1</u>** – 9 + **<u>1</u>** = ___ – ___ = ___ Add **<u>1</u>** to each number.

b) 13 – 7 = ___ + ___ – ___ + ___ = ___ – ___ = ___ Add ___ to each number.

c) 17 – 8 = ___ + ___ – ___ + ___ = ___ – ___ = ___ Add ___ to each number.

d) 18 – 9 = ___ + ___ – ___ + ___ = ___ – ___ = ___ Add ___ to each number.

e) 43 – 6 = Add ___ to each number.

f) 34 – 5 = Add ___ to each number.

g) 26 – 7 = Add ___ to each number.

Taking Apart to Make Tens for Subtraction (continued)

23 – 18 = 23 + **2** – 18 + **2** = 25 – 20 = 5
18 + 2 = 20 So, add 2 to each number.

2. Make an easier problem using 10. Then subtract.

a) 34 – 17 = ___ + ___ – ___ + ___ = ___ – ___ = ___ Add ___ to each number.

b) 28 – 19 = ___ + ___ – ___ + ___ = ___ – ___ = ___ Add ___ to each number.

c) 22 – 16 = ___ + ___ – ___ + ___ = ___ – ___ = ___ Add ___ to each number.

d) 34 – 15 = ___ + ___ – ___ + ___ = ___ – ___ = ___ Add ___ to each number.

e) 43 – 35 = Add ___ to each number.

f) 51 – 39 = Add ___ to each number.

g) 35 – 26 = Add ___ to each number.

Math Riddle

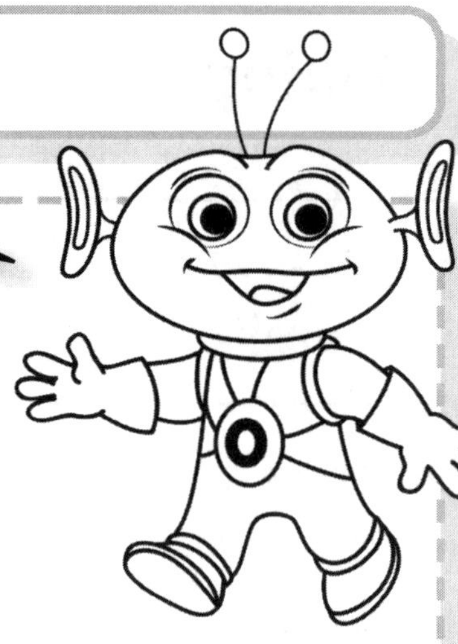

Why did the alien throw his tea?

___ ___ / ___ ___ ___ ___ ___ ___ / ___ ___ /
35 42 / 25 40 63 100 42 48 / 100 70 /

___ ___ ___ / ___ / ___ ___ ___ ___ ___ ___ /
56 42 42 / 40 / 81 18 27 20 63 72 /

___ ___ ___ ___ ___ ___ !
56 40 90 36 42 45 !

A	C	D	E	F	G
130 − 90	19 + 17	207 − 159	84 − 42	36 + 45	56 + 16
H	**I**	**L**	**N**	**O**	**R**
40 − 5	11 + 9	36 − 18	100 − 37	45 + 25	50 − 5
S	**T**	**U**	**W**	**Y**	
100 − 44	13 + 87	45 + 45	75 − 50	30 − 3	

Three-Digit Subtraction Without Regrouping

Line up the ones, tens, and hundreds.

Subtract the ones.

	hundreds	tens	ones
	4	8	7
−	1	4	4
			3

Then subtract the tens.

	hundreds	tens	ones
	4	8	7
−	1	4	4
		4	3

Then subtract the hundreds.

	hundreds	tens	ones
	4	8	7
−	1	4	4
	3	4	3

1. Use a hundreds, tens, and ones chart to help subtract. Shade the ones column yellow. Shade the tens column orange. Shade the hundreds column green.

659 − 111	577 − 243	429 − 15	474 − 131	833 − 302

659 − 111	577 − 243	429 − 15	474 − 131	833 − 302
778 − 223	986 − 432	575 − 372	357 − 226	965 − 524
879 − 127	468 − 241	437 − 315	247 − 137	539 − 536
482 − 31	843 − 742	348 − 328	575 − 424	433 − 122

Three-Digit Subtraction Without Regrouping (continued)

2. Use the hundreds, tens, and ones chart to subtract.

245 − 233 = ____	736 − 121 = ____	278 − 134 = ____	138 − 115 = ____	695 − 530 = ____
867 − 30 = ____	387 − 132 = ____	945 − 330 = ____	253 − 20 = ____	483 − 71 = ____
224 − 111 = ____	552 − 341 = ____	467 − 362 = ____	859 − 723 = ____	775 − 350 = ____
449 − 204 = ____	199 − 155 = ____	786 − 342 = ____	577 − 224 = ____	975 − 322 = ____

BRAIN STRETCH

Use blocks to subtract 3238 – 1255. Draw a picture to show your work.

Three-Digit Subtraction with Regrouping

Line up the ones, tens, and hundreds.
Subtract the ones.

Trade 1 hundred from the hundreds for 10 tens in the tens column.
Subtract the tens.
Then subtract the hundreds.

	hundreds	tens	ones
	5	14	
	~~6~~	~~4~~	6
−	3	8	3
	2	6	3

You cannot take 8 from 4. So, trade 1 hundred from the hundreds for 10 tens. Now there are 14 tens.

1. Use a hundreds, tens and ones chart to help subtract. Shade the ones column yellow. Shade the tens column orange. Shade the hundreds column green.

556 − 275 = ___	418 − 136 = ___	735 − 263 = ___	856 − 283 = ___	529 − 237 = ___
428 − 158 = ___	565 − 185 = ___	634 − 491 = ___	748 − 497 = ___	414 − 240 = ___
853 − 371 = ___	989 − 396 = ___	525 − 255 = ___	874 − 380 = ___	641 − 180 = ___

Three-Digit Subtraction with Regrouping (continued)

2. Use the hundreds, tens, and ones chart to subtract. You will need to regroup the tens.

□ 3 10	□□□	□□□	□□□	□□□
4 4 0 (4 0 crossed out)	4 8 0	3 6 5	3 4 2	8 9 1
− 1 2 9	− 1 8 5	− 1 3 8	− 1 2 5	− 1 7 8
3 1 1	____	____	____	____

□□□	□□□	□□□	□□□	□□□
6 9 1	5 4 0	5 4 0	3 5 3	3 8 0
− 3 6 6	− 1 1 8	− 1 3 4	− 2 3 5	− 1 2 9
____	____	____	____	____

□□□	□□□	□□□	□□□	□□□
8 7 3	3 5 2	6 9 3	2 9 2	5 5 7
− 1 2 4	− 1 3 8	− 6 5 6	− 1 3 6	− 3 1 9
____	____	____	____	____

3. Subtract. Regroup where necessary.

□□□	□□□	□□□	□□□	□□□
4 2 6	6 3 8	7 5 3	3 4 0	6 2 2
− 1 8 1	− 3 7 4	− 3 2 6	− 1 4 7	− 2 7 6
____	____	____	____	____

Four-Digit Subtraction with Regrouping

Line up the ones, tens, hundreds, and thousands.
Subtract the ones. Subtract the tens.

Trade 1 thousand from the thousands for 10 hundreds in the hundreds column. Subtract the hundreds and then the thousands.

	thousands	hundreds	tens	ones
	4	16		
	~~5~~	~~6~~	9	6
−	2	8	8	3
	2	8	1	3

You cannot take 8 from 6. So, trade 1 thousand from the thousands for 10 hundreds. Now there are 16 hundreds.

1. Subtract by regrouping where needed. Use a place value chart to help you. Shade the ones column yellow, the tens column orange, the hundreds column green, and the thousands column blue.

$$\begin{array}{r} 4186 \\ -\,2275 \\ \hline \end{array} \quad \begin{array}{r} 6317 \\ -\,3136 \\ \hline \end{array} \quad \begin{array}{r} 4635 \\ -\,3264 \\ \hline \end{array} \quad \begin{array}{r} 5556 \\ -\,4293 \\ \hline \end{array} \quad \begin{array}{r} 5249 \\ -\,3837 \\ \hline \end{array}$$

$$\begin{array}{r} 3238 \\ -\,1158 \\ \hline \end{array} \quad \begin{array}{r} 6590 \\ -\,4385 \\ \hline \end{array} \quad \begin{array}{r} 3394 \\ -\,1494 \\ \hline \end{array} \quad \begin{array}{r} 4398 \\ -\,2487 \\ \hline \end{array} \quad \begin{array}{r} 7481 \\ -\,3242 \\ \hline \end{array}$$

Hint: Regroup in more than one column.

$$\begin{array}{r} 8293 \\ -\,5776 \\ \hline \end{array} \quad \begin{array}{r} 4789 \\ -\,3296 \\ \hline \end{array} \quad \begin{array}{r} 9215 \\ -\,6755 \\ \hline \end{array} \quad \begin{array}{r} 3474 \\ -\,1883 \\ \hline \end{array} \quad \begin{array}{r} 5471 \\ -\,1654 \\ \hline \end{array}$$

Subtraction Match

Match the question and the answer.

Question	Answer
2345 − 2131	1396
8398 − 52	4644
1697 − 301	8346
5028 − 1213	903
1473 − 120	1353
1138 − 235	6731
7079 − 348	3815
4804 − 160	214

Word Problems

Solve each problem.

1. Sandra has 329 stamps. Dave has 76 more stamps than Sandra.

   a) How many stamps does Dave have? ______________

   b) How many stamps are there in total? ______________

2. Ms. Steven's class raised $425 for a school trip. Mr. Kerem's class raised $548.

   a) Whose class raised more money? ______________________

   b) How much more money did the class raise? ____________________

3. At a camp, 238 children enrolled in swimming. There are 56 more children enrolled in canoeing than swimming.

   a) How many children are enrolled in canoeing? ____________

   b) How many children are enrolled in swimming and canoeing altogether? ____________

4. Michael's hockey team sold 1329 tickets for the hockey tournament. Shelly's team sold 1267 tickets more than Michael's team.

   a) How many tickets were sold altogether? ___________

   b) How many tickets did Shelly's team sell? ___________

Money Riddle

When does it rain money?

w	h	e	n	t	h	e	r	e
$1.25	$3.00	$2.00	$2.50	50¢	$3.00	$2.00	$1.20	$2.00

i	s	c	h	a	n	g	e
25¢	$1.50	$2.35	$3.00	$1.00	$2.50	75¢	$2.00

i	n	t	h	e
25¢	$2.50	50¢	$3.00	$2.00

w	e	a	t	h	e	r
$1.25	$2.00	$1.00	50¢	$3.00	$2.00	$1.20

A	C	E	G
 $1.00	 $2.35	 $2.00	 75¢
H	**I**	**N**	**R**
 $3.00	 25¢	 $2.50	 $1.20
S	**T**	**W**	**Y**
 $1.50	 50¢	 $1.25	 $4.00

Counting with Bills and Coins

Draw the bills and coins needed to make the total.

1. 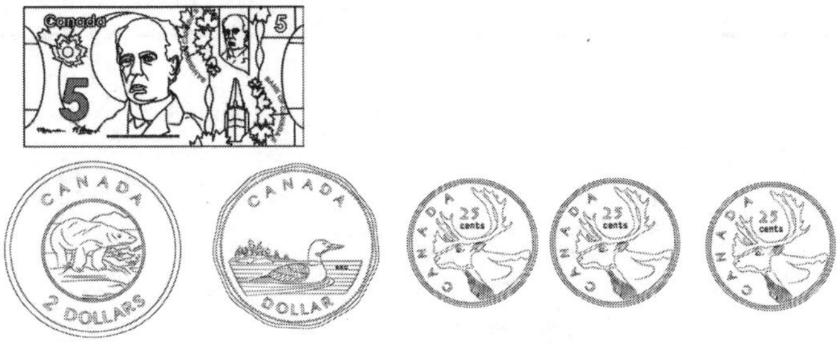

$ 8.75 ________

2. $ 25.85 ________

3. $ 10.00 ________

4. $ 17.55 ________

5. $ 16.20 ________

Comparing Money Values

1. Compare and write >, <, or = in the ◯.

a)

What is the value? ______________

What is the value? ______________

b)

What is the value? ______________

What is the value? ______________

c)

What is the value? ______________

What is the value? ______________

Patterns on a 100 Chart

1. Shade number patterns.

- Use blue to show counting by 3s. Use green to show counting by 4s.
- Use circles to show counting by 6s. Use squares to show counting by 8s.

1	2	3	4	5	6	7	8	9	10
11	12	13	14	15	16	17	18	19	20
21	22	23	24	25	26	27	28	29	30
31	32	33	34	35	36	37	38	39	40
41	42	43	44	45	46	47	48	49	50
51	52	53	54	55	56	57	58	59	60
61	62	63	64	65	66	67	68	69	70
71	72	73	74	75	76	77	78	79	80
81	82	83	84	85	86	87	88	89	90
91	92	93	94	95	96	97	98	99	100

2. What do you notice about the ones digit:

a) when counting by 3s? ____________________

b) when counting by 6s? ____________________

c) when counting by 4s? ____________________

d) when counting by 8s? ____________________

3. What kinds of vertical, horizontal, or diagonal patterns do you see:

a) when counting by 3s? __________________________________

b) when counting by 4s? __________________________________

Arrays

In the **array**, there are 2 rows with 4 blocks in each row.
Skip count by 4s to count the blocks.
The multiplication statement is 2 × 4 = 8.

1. Write a multiplication statement for each array.

 **2** rows and **3** blocks in each row **2 × 3 = 6**

a)  ___ rows and ___ blocks in each row __________

b)  ___ rows and ___ blocks in each row __________

c)  ___ rows and ___ blocks in each row __________

2. Write a multiplication statement for each array.

a)  __________

b)  __________

c)  __________

d)  __________

e)  __________

f)  __________

Arrays (continued)

3. Draw an array for each. Write the multiplication statement.

a) 5 × 4

b) 4 × 8

c) 1 × 6

d) 2 × 9

e) 4 × 4

f) 6 × 3

g) 6 × 6

h) 7 × 1

i) 3 × 2

j) 7 × 4

k) 2 × 10

l) 3 × 5

Using Doubles to Multiply

If you know 2 times a number, you can double to find 4 times the number.

For 4 × 6, you know:

2 × 6 = 12

Double 2 to get 4. Double the product to get 24.

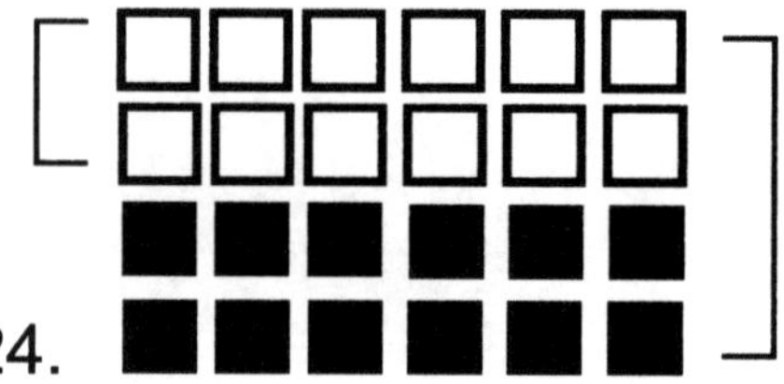

So, 4 × 6 = **24**.

1. Use doubles to multiply. Draw an array to help.

a) 2 × 7 = ___

So 4 × 7 = ____

b) 2 × 8 = ___

So 4 × 8 = ___

c) 2 × 5 = ___

So 4 × 5 = ___

d) 2 × 9 = ___

So 4 × 9 = ___

e) 3 × 5 = ___

So 6 × 5 = ___

f) 3 × 6 = ___

So 6 × 6 = ___

2. Use doubling to solve each problem.

a) 2 stamps each cost 55¢

b) 4 balls each cost 80¢

c) 8 stickers each cost 12¢

Using Doubles to Multiply (continued)

3. Use repeated doubles to multiply. Hint: Double 2 times the number to find 4 times the number. Then double to find 8 times the number.

2 × 6 = **12** so 4 × 6 = **24** and 8 × 6 = 48

a) 2 × 8 = ___ so 4 × 8 = ___ and 8 × 8 = ___

b) 2 × 7 = ___ so 4 × 7 = ___ and 8 × 7 = ___

4. Molly finds the multiplication facts for 6 by doubling the multiplication facts for 3. Does Molly's strategy work? Use numbers, words, and pictures to show how you know.

5. Double 3 times the number to find 6 times the number. Then double to find 12 times the number.

a) 3 × 3 = ___ so 6 × 3 = ___ and 12 × 3 = ___

b) 3 × 8 = ___ so 6 × 8 = ___ and 12 × 8 = ___

BRAIN STRETCH

Use repeated doubles to find 16 times a number. Hint: Use 2 times, 4 times, 8 times and 16 times.

a) 3

b) 5

Multiply by Adding a Group

For 3 × 7, you know that 3 × 7 is one more group than 2 × 7.
Use multiplication and addition to solve the problems.

3 × 7 =	**2 × 7**	**+ 7**
three 7s	two 7s	and one more 7

So 3 × 7 = 2 × 7 + 7
= 14 + 7
= 21

Use multiplication and addition to solve the problems.

Find the product.

1. 3 × 6 = **2** × **6** + 6 = _____ + _____ = _____

2. 5 × 4 = ______________________________

3. 6 × 5 = ______________________________

4. 5 × 7 = ______________________________

5. 7 × 6 = ______________________________

6. 9 × 4 = ______________________________

Multiplying by 4, 5, and 6

Use an array to help find the product.

9×4 = 36	2×4 = 8	5×6 = 30	2×6 = 12	3×5 = 15
7×5 = 35	5×4 = 20	1×6 = 6	0×5 = 0	6×4 = 24
4×5 = 20	3×6 = 18	8×5 = 40	1×4 = 4	4×6 = 24
0×4 = 0	9×6 = 54	2×5 = 10	6×6 = 36	5×5 = 25

BRAIN STRETCH

Beth made a photo album. The photo album had 8 pages. Each page had 7 pictures. How many pictures were in the photo album altogether? Draw an array to show your work. 8 x 7 =

Using Patterns to Multiply by 9

Use the ten facts to help multiply by 9.
For 9 × 6, you know that 10 × 6 is one more group than 9 × 6.

9 × 6 =	60	–	6
nine 6s	ten 6s	–	one 6

So 9 × 6 = 54

1. Use the ten facts to help multiply by 9. Show your work.

a) 9 × 3

b) 9 × 7

2. a) Use the pattern in the tens and ones digits to help learn the nine facts.

1 × 9 = ____ **9**
2 × 9 = **1** **8**
3 × 9 = **2** **7**
4 × 9 = ____ ____
5 × 9 = ____ ____
6 × 9 = ____ ____
7 × 9 = ____ ____
8 × 9 = ____ ____
9 × 9 = ____ ____
10 × 9 = ____ ____

b) What pattern do you notice about the nine facts?

Multiplying by 7, 8, and 9

Use an array to help find the product.

$9 \times 9 =$ ____	$1 \times 9 =$ ____	$4 \times 7 =$ ____	$2 \times 7 =$ ____	$5 \times 8 =$ ____
$4 \times 8 =$ ____	$2 \times 9 =$ ____	$1 \times 7 =$ ____	$3 \times 8 =$ ____	$6 \times 9 =$ ____
$8 \times 8 =$ ____	$3 \times 7 =$ ____	$0 \times 8 =$ ____	$5 \times 9 =$ ____	$9 \times 7 =$ ____
$0 \times 9 =$ ____	$7 \times 7 =$ ____	$2 \times 8 =$ ____	$5 \times 7 =$ ____	$6 \times 7 =$ ____

BRAIN STRETCH

Bill says that the product of 8 × 9 is the same as the product of 9 × 8. Is he correct? Show how you know.

Match-Up Fun

Write each sum and product. Then match the sum to the product.

7 + 7 + 7 + 7 + 7 + 7 = ______	6 × 4 = ______
8 + 8 + 8 + 8 + 8 + 8 + 8 = ______	9 × 6 = ______
7 + 7 + 7 + 7 + 7 + 7 + 7 = ______	8 × 6 = ______
9 + 9 + 9 + 9 + 9 + 9 + 9 + 9 = ______	5 × 9 = ______
4 + 4 + 4 + 4 + 4 + 4 = ______	7 × 6 = ______
6 + 6 + 6 + 6 + 6 + 6 + 6 + 6 + 6 = ______	9 × 7 = ______
6 + 6 + 6 + 6 + 6 + 6 + 6 + 6 = ______	8 × 5 = ______
6 + 6 + 6 + 6 = ______	7 × 7 = ______
9 + 9 + 9 + 9 + 9 = ______	8 × 9 = ______
5 + 5 + 5 + 5 + 5 + 5 + 5 = ______	6 × 7 = ______
8 + 8 + 8 + 8 + 8 + 8 + 8 + 8 + 8 = ______	7 × 8 = ______
6 + 6 + 6 + 6 + 6 + 6 + 6 = ______	6 × 5 = ______
7 + 7 + 7 + 7 + 7 + 7 + 7 + 7 + 7 = ______	9 × 8 = ______
5 + 5 + 5 + 5 + 5 + 5 = ______	4 × 6 = ______
5 + 5 + 5 + 5 + 5 + 5 + 5 + 5 = ______	7 × 5 = ______

Hint: The answer in addition is called the **sum**.
The answer in multiplication is called the **product**.

Multiplication Fact Fun

Multiply.

1. 1 × 2 = 2
2. 3 × 6 = 18
3. 5 × 7 = 35
4. 6 × 9 = 54
5. 9 × 0 = 0
6. 8 × 6 = ______
7. 2 × 8 = ______
8. 7 × 6 = ______
9. 4 × 4 = ______
10. 9 × 2 = ______
11. 7 × 3 = ______
12. 5 × 1 = ______
13. 3 × 0 = ______
14. 9 × 3 = ______
15. 8 × 8 = ______
16. 4 × 7 = ______
17. 2 × 4 = ______
18. 6 × 8 = ______
19. 9 × 9 = ______
20. 2 × 7 = ______
21. 5 × 6 = ______
22. 9 × 4 = ______
23. 8 × 2 = ______
24. 7 × 5 = ______
25. 0 × 6 = ______
26. 3 × 3 = ______
27. 4 × 1 = ______
28. 1 × 9 = ______
29. 2 × 5 = ______
30. 4 × 0 = ______
31. 6 × 6 = ______
32. 8 × 4 = ______
33. 9 × 5 = ______
34. 3 × 9 = ______
35. 1 × 5 = ______
36. 5 × 8 = ______
37. 7 × 7 = ______
38. 8 × 3 = ______

Multiplication Fact Fun (continued)

Multiply.

1. $8 \times 2 =$ ______
2. $9 \times 3 =$ ______
3. $10 \times 5 =$ ______
4. $1 \times 0 =$ ______
5. $2 \times 6 =$ ______
6. $3 \times 7 =$ ______
7. $6 \times 4 =$ ______
8. $6 \times 7 =$ ______
9. $2 \times 3 =$ ______
10. $4 \times 9 =$ ______
11. $6 \times 11 =$ ______
12. $3 \times 5 =$ ______
13. $5 \times 5 =$ ______
14. $4 \times 5 =$ ______
15. $9 \times 8 =$ ______
16. $2 \times 2 =$ ______
17. $7 \times 4 =$ ______
18. $2 \times 7 =$ ______
19. $6 \times 3 =$ ______
20. $7 \times 9 =$ ______
21. $8 \times 7 =$ ______
22. $9 \times 1 =$ ______
23. $7 \times 2 =$ ______
24. $4 \times 6 =$ ______
25. $6 \times 2 =$ ______
26. $9 \times 7 =$ ______
27. $6 \times 9 =$ ______
28. $8 \times 5 =$ ______
29. $4 \times 3 =$ ______
30. $5 \times 3 =$ ______
31. $6 \times 5 =$ ______
32. $1 \times 6 =$ ______
33. $7 \times 0 =$ ______
34. $3 \times 8 =$ ______
35. $2 \times 1 =$ ______
36. $9 \times 6 =$ ______
37. $7 \times 1 =$ ______
38. $7 \times 8 =$ ______

Multiply Numbers by Tens

You can multiply by tens using tens blocks.
2 × 30 =

Make 2 groups of 3 tens.

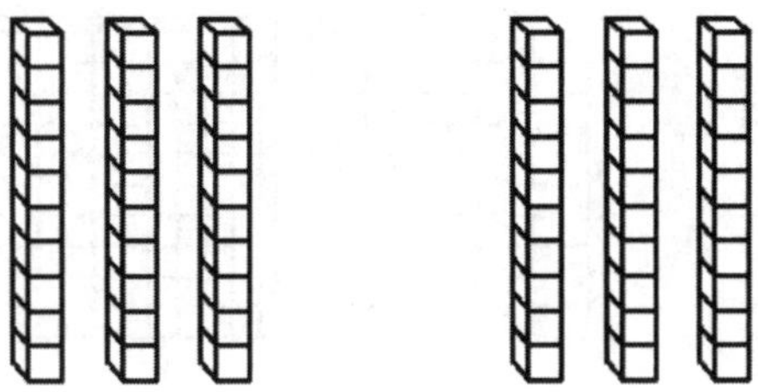

2 × 30 = 2 × 3 tens = 6 tens = 60 So, 2 × 30 = 60

What pattern do you see? 2 × 3 = 6

2 × 30 = 60

1. Draw tens blocks. Then multiply.

a) 2 × 40 = ____ **b)** 3 × 20 = ____

2. Use the pattern to multiply.

a) 5 × 1 = ____ **b)** 6 × 2 = ____ **c)** 7 × 3 = ____

5 × 10 = ____ 6 × 20 = ____ 7 × 30 = ____

Multiply Numbers by Hundreds

You can multiply by hundreds using hundreds blocks.
3 × 200 =

Make 3 groups of 2 hundreds.

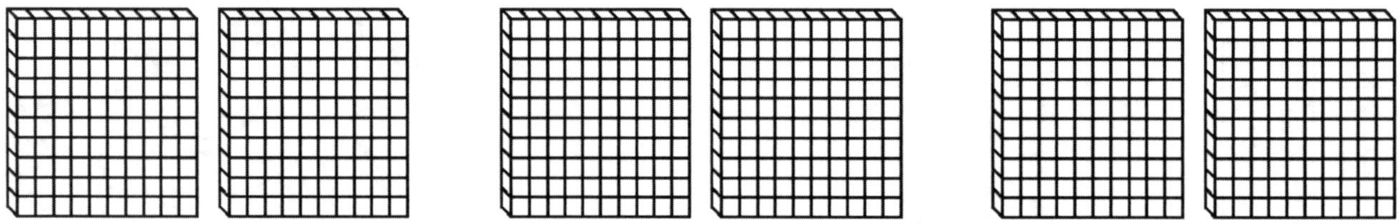

3 × 200 = 3 × 2 hundreds = 6 hundreds = 600 So, 3 × 200 = 600

What pattern do you see?

3 × 2 = 6
3 × 20 = 60
3 × 200 = 600

1. Draw hundreds blocks. Then multiply.

a) 3 × 300 = ____ **b)** 4 × 200 = ____

2. Use the pattern to multiply.

a) 4 × 6 = ____
4 × 60 = ____
4 × 600 = ____

b) 8 × 5 = ____
8 × 50 = ____
8 × 500 = ____

c) 9 × 4 = ____
9 × 40 = ____
9 × 400 = ____

Multiply Numbers by Thousands

You can multiply by thousands using thousands blocks.
4 × 2000 =

Make 4 groups of 2 thousands.

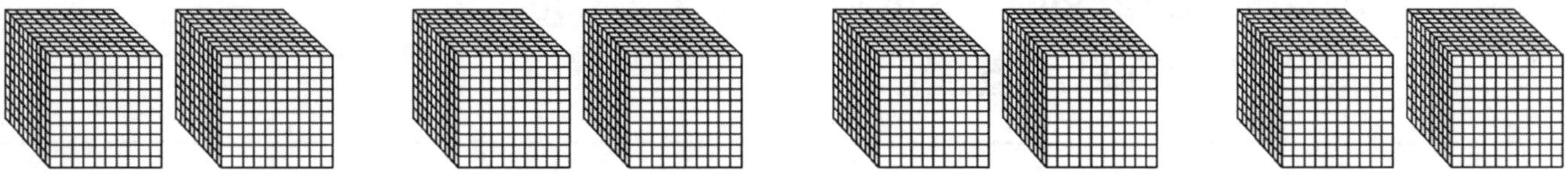

4 × 2000 = 4 × 2 thousands = 8 thousands = 8000   So, 4 × 2000 = 8000

What pattern do you see?

4 × 2 = 8
4 × 20 = 80
4 × 200 = 800
4 × 2000 = 8000

1. Draw thousands blocks. Then multiply.

a) 2 × 2000 = ____

b) 3 × 3000 = ____

c) 5 × 1000 = ____

d) 3 × 4000 = ____

Multiply Multiples of 10, 100, and 1000

Multiply $7 \times 5000 =$ ______

7×5 ones = 35 ones = **35**

7×5 tens = 35 tens = **350**

7×5 hundreds = 35 hundreds = **3500**

7×5 thousands = 35 thousands = **35 000**

So $7 \times 5000 =$ **35 000**

1. Use multiplication facts and patterns to help multiply.

a) $2 \times 6 =$ ______

$2 \times 60 =$ ______

$2 \times 600 =$ ______

$2 \times 6000 =$ ______

b) $4 \times 7 =$ ______

$4 \times 70 =$ ______

$4 \times 700 =$ ______

$4 \times 7000 =$ ______

c) $3 \times 3 =$ ______

$3 \times 30 =$ ______

$3 \times 300 =$ ______

$3 \times 3000 =$ ______

d) $5 \times 6 =$ ______

$5 \times 60 =$ ______

$5 \times 600 =$ ______

$5 \times 6000 =$ ______

e) $8 \times 2 =$ ______

$8 \times 20 =$ ______

$8 \times 200 =$ ______

$8 \times 2000 =$ ______

f) $9 \times 4 =$ ______

$9 \times 40 =$ ______

$9 \times 400 =$ ______

$9 \times 4000 =$ ______

g) $2 \times 7 =$ ______

$2 \times 70 =$ ______

$2 \times 700 =$ ______

$2 \times 7000 =$ ______

h) $3 \times 5 =$ ______

$3 \times 50 =$ ______

$3 \times 500 =$ ______

$3 \times 5000 =$ ______

I) $7 \times 6 =$ ______

$7 \times 60 =$ ______

$7 \times 600 =$ ______

$7 \times 6000 =$ ______

Multiply Multiples of 10, 100, and 1000 (continued)

2. Use the pattern to multiply.

a) 2 × 3 = ____

2 × 30 = ____

2 × 300 = ____

2 × 3000 = ____

b) 2 × 2 = ____

2 × 20 = ____

2 × 200 = ____

2 × 2000 = ____

c) 2 × 4 = ____

2 × 40 = ____

2 × 400 = ____

2 × 4000 = ____

3. Multiply.

a) 2 × 50 = ____

b) 3 × 400 = ____

c) 4 × 1000 = ____

d) 5 × 200 = ____

e) 6 × 40 = ____

f) 7 × 300 = ____

g) 6 × 300 = ____

h) 5 × 60 = ____

i) 8 × 500 = ____

Multiply Two-Digit Numbers by One-Digit Numbers

Step 1: Multiply the ones.

6 ones × 9 ones = 54 ones
Regroup 54 as 5 tens and 4 ones.

$$\begin{array}{r} \boxed{5} \\ 16 \\ \times\ 9 \\ \hline 4 \end{array}$$

Step 2: Multiply the tens.

1 ten × 9 ones = 9 tens
Then add the regrouped 5 tens.
9 tens + 5 tens = 14 tens

$$\begin{array}{r} \boxed{5} \\ 16 \\ \times\ 9 \\ \hline 144 \end{array}$$

1 hundred + 4 tens + 4 ones

Multiply.

1. $\begin{array}{r} 37 \\ \times\ 2 \\ \hline \end{array}$

2. $\begin{array}{r} 14 \\ \times\ 4 \\ \hline \end{array}$

3. $\begin{array}{r} 82 \\ \times\ 5 \\ \hline \end{array}$

4. $\begin{array}{r} 73 \\ \times\ 2 \\ \hline \end{array}$

5. $\begin{array}{r} 15 \\ \times\ 5 \\ \hline \end{array}$

6. $\begin{array}{r} 35 \\ \times\ 3 \\ \hline \end{array}$

7. $\begin{array}{r} 57 \\ \times\ 4 \\ \hline \end{array}$

8. $\begin{array}{r} 46 \\ \times\ 3 \\ \hline \end{array}$

9. $\begin{array}{r} 19 \\ \times\ 3 \\ \hline \end{array}$

10. $\begin{array}{r} 26 \\ \times\ 2 \\ \hline \end{array}$

11. $\begin{array}{r} 43 \\ \times\ 5 \\ \hline \end{array}$

12. $\begin{array}{r} 82 \\ \times\ 4 \\ \hline \end{array}$

Multiply Two-Digit Numbers by One-Digit Numbers (continued)

Multiply. Hint: Make sure to line up the numbers.

13. $15 \times 2 =$ ____

14. $52 \times 4 =$ ____

15. $41 \times 5 =$ ____

16. $23 \times 2 =$ ____

17. $94 \times 4 =$ ____

18. $26 \times 5 =$ ____

19. $67 \times 2 =$ ____

20. $84 \times 3 =$ ____

21. $97 \times 2 =$ ____

22. $18 \times 7 =$ ____

23. $47 \times 5 =$ ____

24. $16 \times 9 =$ ____

25. $34 \times 8 =$ ____

26. $29 \times 7 =$ ____

27. $58 \times 6 =$ ____

28. $76 \times 3 =$ ____

29. $24 \times 9 =$ ____

30. $62 \times 2 =$ ____

31. $75 \times 6 =$ ____

32. $33 \times 8 =$ ____

Multiply Two-Digit Numbers by One-Digit Numbers (continued)

Multiply. Hint: Make sure to line up the numbers.

33.
$$\begin{array}{r} 24 \\ \times \quad 4 \\ \hline \\ \hline \end{array}$$

34.
$$\begin{array}{r} 96 \\ \times \quad 2 \\ \hline \\ \hline \end{array}$$

35.
$$\begin{array}{r} 46 \\ \times \quad 3 \\ \hline \\ \hline \end{array}$$

36.
$$\begin{array}{r} 84 \\ \times \quad 5 \\ \hline \\ \hline \end{array}$$

37.
$$\begin{array}{r} 44 \\ \times \quad 8 \\ \hline \\ \hline \end{array}$$

38.
$$\begin{array}{r} 55 \\ \times \quad 6 \\ \hline \\ \hline \end{array}$$

39.
$$\begin{array}{r} 37 \\ \times \quad 2 \\ \hline \\ \hline \end{array}$$

40.
$$\begin{array}{r} 26 \\ \times \quad 7 \\ \hline \\ \hline \end{array}$$

41.
$$\begin{array}{r} 74 \\ \times \quad 5 \\ \hline \\ \hline \end{array}$$

42.
$$\begin{array}{r} 35 \\ \times \quad 4 \\ \hline \\ \hline \end{array}$$

43.
$$\begin{array}{r} 55 \\ \times \quad 3 \\ \hline \\ \hline \end{array}$$

44.
$$\begin{array}{r} 66 \\ \times \quad 2 \\ \hline \\ \hline \end{array}$$

BRAIN STRETCH

Katie walks a total of 6 km a day going to and from school. She goes to school for 189 days per year. What is the total distance Katie walks back and forth to school in one year?

Multiply Multi-Digit Numbers

Step 1:
Multiply the ones.
6 ones × 5 ones
= 30 ones

Regroup 30 as
3 tens and 0 ones.

$$\begin{array}{r} \boxed{3} \\ 316 \\ \times \quad 5 \\ \hline 0 \\ \hline \end{array}$$

Step 2:
Multiply the tens.
1 ten × 5 ones
= 5 tens

Then add the
regrouped 3 tens.
5 tens + 3 tens
= 8 tens

$$\begin{array}{r} \boxed{3} \\ 316 \\ \times \quad 5 \\ \hline 80 \\ \hline \end{array}$$

Step 3:
Multiply the hundreds.
3 hundreds × 5 ones
= 15 hundreds

Regroup 1500 as
1 thousand and
5 hundreds.

$$\begin{array}{r} \boxed{3} \\ 316 \\ \times \quad 5 \\ \hline 1580 \\ \hline \end{array}$$

Since there are no other thousands, write the "1" in the answer.

Multiply. Regroup where necessary.

1.
$$\begin{array}{r} 237 \\ \times \quad 3 \\ \hline \\ \hline \end{array}$$

2.
$$\begin{array}{r} 314 \\ \times \quad 2 \\ \hline \\ \hline \end{array}$$

3.
$$\begin{array}{r} 182 \\ \times \quad 5 \\ \hline \\ \hline \end{array}$$

4.
$$\begin{array}{r} 373 \\ \times \quad 4 \\ \hline \\ \hline \end{array}$$

5.
$$\begin{array}{r} 215 \\ \times \quad 5 \\ \hline \\ \hline \end{array}$$

6.
$$\begin{array}{r} 135 \\ \times \quad 3 \\ \hline \\ \hline \end{array}$$

7.
$$\begin{array}{r} 257 \\ \times \quad 4 \\ \hline \\ \hline \end{array}$$

8.
$$\begin{array}{r} 346 \\ \times \quad 6 \\ \hline \\ \hline \end{array}$$

Multiply Multi-Digit Numbers (continued)

Multiply. Regroup where necessary.

9. $319 \times 6 = $ ______

10. $526 \times 3 = $ ______

11. $443 \times 4 = $ ______

12. $282 \times 5 = $ ______

13. $115 \times 2 = $ ______

14. $325 \times 4 = $ ______

15. $411 \times 5 = $ ______

16. $233 \times 3 = $ ______

17. $914 \times 9 = $ ______

18. $526 \times 5 = $ ______

19. $627 \times 8 = $ ______

20. $824 \times 6 = $ ______

21. $2347 \times 2 = $ ______

22. $1218 \times 3 = $ ______

23. $2811 \times 5 = $ ______

24. $3162 \times 4 = $ ______

25. $2134 \times 8 = $ ______

26. $1523 \times 7 = $ ______

27. $2351 \times 6 = $ ______

28. $4116 \times 5 = $ ______

Estimate a Product

To estimate, round at least one **factor** to make it easier to multiply.
The factors are the numbers you multiply together.

Rounding one factor:
Estimate: 7 × 91   Round 91 to 100.

Think: For 7 × 100, you know that 7 × 10 = 70. Add one zero to multiply by 100.
The estimated product is 7 × 100 = 700.

1. Estimate by rounding one factor. Show your work.
Hint: Round to the nearest ten or the nearest hundred.

a) 3 × 59   **b)** 11 × 48   **c)** 6 × 415

d) 6 × 99   **e)** 8 × 35   **f)** 50 × 79

g) 9 × 18   **h)** 60 × 49   **i)** 40 × 94

Estimate a Product (continued)

Rounding both factors:
Estimate: 32 × 67 Round both factors. 32 is close to 30 and 67 is close to 70.

Think: For 30 × 70, you know that 3 × 7 = 21. Add the zeros from 30 and 70.
The estimated product is 30 × 70 = 2100.

2. Estimate by rounding both factors. Show your work.

a) 25 × 32 **b)** 37 × 59 **c)** 43 × 78

d) 51 × 49 **e)** 68 × 41 **f)** 73 × 28

g) 53 × 635 **h)** 28 × 229 **i)** 46 × 482

BRAIN STRETCH

A bus for a field trip can seat 48 students. How many buses are needed for 287 students?

a) Estimate.

b) Calculate.

Relating Addition and Division

Fill in the missing numbers.

1. $6 + 6 + 6 + 6 =$ ______ ______ $\div 6 = 4$
   ______ groups of the number ______

2. $5 + 5 + 5 + 5 + 5 + 5 + 5 =$ ______ ______ $\div 5 = 7$
   ______ groups of the number ______

3. $9 + 9 + 9 + 9 + 9 + 9 + 9 =$ ______ ______ $\div 9 = 7$
   ______ groups of the number ______

4. $10 + 10 + 10 =$ ______ $30 \div$ ______ $= 3$
   ______ groups of the number ______

5. $7 + 7 + 7 + 7 =$ ______ ______ $\div 4 = 7$
   ______ groups of the number ______

6. $9 + 9 + 9 + 9 + 9 + 9 =$ ______ $54 \div 6 =$ ______
   ______ groups of the number ______

7. $8 + 8 + 8 + 8 + 8 + 8 + 8 + 8 + 8 =$ ______ ______ $\div 8 = 9$
   ______ groups of the number ______

8. $7 + 7 + 7 + 7 + 7 + 7 =$ ______ ______ $\div 7 = 6$
   ______ groups of the number ______

9. $8 + 8 + 8 + 8 + 8 + 8 =$ ______ ______ $\div 8 = 6$
   ______ groups of the number ______

10. $6 + 6 + 6 + 6 + 6 + 6 + 6 + 6 + 6 =$ ______ $54 \div 9 =$ ______
    ______ groups of the number ______

Related Facts

Fill in the missing number.

$5 \times 6 = 30$

$30 \div 6 =$ ________

$9 \times 2 = 18$

$18 \div 2 =$ ________

$8 \times 5 = 40$

$40 \div 5 =$ ________

$9 \times 3 = 27$

$27 \div 9 =$ ________

$7 \times 4 = 28$

$28 \div 4 =$ ________

$8 \times 6 = 48$

$48 \div 6 =$ ________

$6 \times 10 = 60$

$60 \div 10 =$ ________

$9 \times 8 = 72$

$72 \div 8 =$ ________

$6 \times$ ________ $= 54$

$54 \div 9 = 6$

$9 \times 5 = 45$

$45 \div$ ________ $= 5$

$7 \times 7 = 49$

________ $\div 7 = 7$

$6 \times 7 = 42$

$42 \div$ ________ $= 6$

$8 \times 7 = 56$

$56 \div 7 =$ ________

$7 \times 9 = 63$

$63 \div 7 =$ ________

$9 \times 9 =$ ________

$81 \div 9 = 9$

$8 \times 8 = 64$

________ $\div 8 = 8$

Related Facts (continued)

Fill in the missing number.

7 × 2 = 14

14 ÷ 7 = ________

9 × 5 = 45

45 ÷ 9 = ________

4 × 9 = 36

36 ÷ 9 = ________

6 × 4 = 24

24 ÷ 6 = ________

6 × 5 = 30

30 ÷ 6 = ________

6 × 3 = 18

18 ÷ 6 = ________

6 × 6 = 36

36 ÷ 6 = ________

8 × 5 = 40

40 ÷ 8 = ________

10 × 6 = 60

60 ÷ 6 = ________

8 × 8 = 64

64 ÷ 8 ________

6 × 1 = 6

6 ÷ 6 = ________

8 × 3 = 24

24 ÷ 3 = ________

6 × 7 = 42

________ ÷ 6 = 7

9 × 6 = 54

54 ÷ ________ = 9

2 × 5 = ________

10 ÷ 5 = 2

2 × 10 = 20

20 ÷ ________ = 2

Related Facts (continued)

Fill in the missing number.

$4 \times 2 = 8$

$8 \div 2 =$ ________

$3 \times 3 = 9$

$9 \div 3 =$ ________

$9 \times 9 = 81$

$81 \div 9 =$ ________

$9 \times 8 = 72$

$72 \div 9 =$ ________

$7 \times 5 = 35$

$35 \div 5 =$ ________

$7 \times 7 = 49$

$49 \div 7 =$ ________

$10 \times 8 = 80$

$80 \div 10 =$ ________

$9 \times 3 = 27$

$27 \div$ ________ $= 9$

$7 \times 9 =$ ________

$63 \div 7 = 9$

$6 \times 8 = 48$

$48 \div 6 =$ ________

$2 \times$ ________ $= 16$

$16 \div 8 = 2$

$7 \times 3 = 21$

________ $\div 7 = 3$

$8 \times 7 = 56$

$56 \div$ ________ $= 8$

$9 \times 1 =$ ________

$9 \div 9 = 1$

$4 \times 4 = 16$

$16 \div 4 =$ ________

$10 \times 9 = 90$

________ $\div 9 = 10$

Use Halving to Divide

For 32 ÷ 4, you know that 4 is 2 × 2.

To divide by 4, divide by 2. 32 ÷ 2 = 16
Then divide by 2 again. 16 ÷ 2 = 8
So, 32 ÷ 4 = **8**

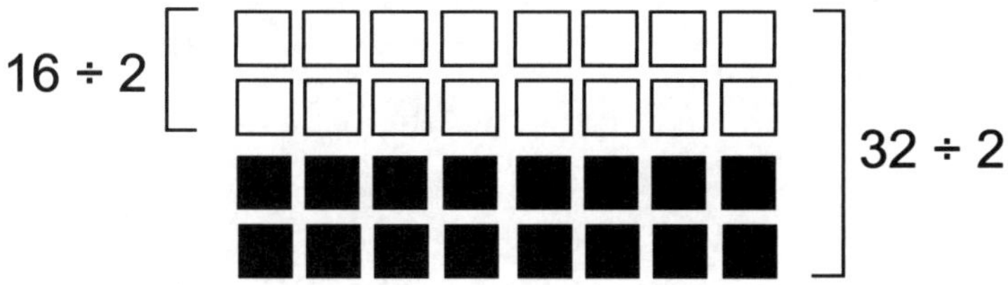

1. Use halving to divide. Draw an array to help.

a) 24 ÷ 4 Divide by 2. ___ Divide by 2 again. ____ So, 24 ÷ 4 = ___

b) 36 ÷ 4 Divide by 2. ___ Divide by 2 again. ____ So, 36 ÷ 4 = ___

c) 40 ÷ 4 Divide by 2. ___ Divide by 2 again. ____ So, 40 ÷ 4 = ___

d) 48 ÷ 4 Divide by 2. ___ Divide by 2 again. ____ So, 48 ÷ 4 = ___

Use Halving to Divide (continued)

2. Use repeated halving to divide.
Hint: To divide by 8, divide by 2, divide by 2, and then divide by 2 again.

a) 16 ÷ 8 Divide by 2. ___ Divide by 2. ___ Divide by 2. _____ So, 16 ÷ 8 = ___

b) 32 ÷ 8 Divide by 2. ___ Divide by 2. ___ Divide by 2. _____ So, 32 ÷ 8 = ___

c) 64 ÷ 8 Divide by 2. ___ Divide by 2. ___ Divide by 2. _____ So, 64 ÷ 8 = ___

d) 48 ÷ 8 Divide by 2. ___ Divide by 2. ___ Divide by 2. _____ So, 48 ÷ 8 = ___

BRAIN STRETCH

Seth says he can use repeated halving to divide 40 ÷ 8? Is he correct?
Show all the steps.

Dividing by 4, 5, and 6

Divide.

$4\overline{)24}$	$5\overline{)5}$	$6\overline{)18}$	$4\overline{)44}$
$6\overline{)60}$	$4\overline{)20}$	$5\overline{)10}$	$6\overline{)30}$
$5\overline{)35}$	$6\overline{)42}$	$4\overline{)4}$	$5\overline{)55}$
$4\overline{)28}$	$5\overline{)20}$	$6\overline{)66}$	$4\overline{)12}$

Dividing by 7, 8, and 9

Divide.

7)49	8)96	8)24	9)18
8)64	9)99	7)56	8)40
7)63	8)56	9)90	7)70
9)54	7)42	8)48	9)27

Division Fact Fun

Divide.

1. 48 ÷ 6 = ______

2. 27 ÷ 3 = ______

3. 6 ÷ 2 = ______

4. 80 ÷ 8 = ______

5. 30 ÷ 3 = ______

6. 18 ÷ 1 = ______

7. 18 ÷ 3 = ______

8. 27 ÷ 9 = ______

9. 56 ÷ 7 = ______

10. 5 ÷ 1 = ______

11. 20 ÷ 4 = ______

12. 25 ÷ 5 = ______

13. 81 ÷ 9 = 9

14. 20 ÷ 5 = 4

15. 72 ÷ 9 = 8

16. 16 ÷ 8 = ______

17. 8 ÷ 2 = 4

18. 18 ÷ 6 = 3

19. 24 ÷ 3 = 8

20. 21 ÷ 7 = ______

21. 36 ÷ 4 = ______

22. 40 ÷ 8 = ______

23. 12 ÷ 6 = ______

24. 90 ÷ 9 = ______

25. 24 ÷ 8 = 3

26. 4 ÷ 2 = 2

27. 40 ÷ 5 = 8

28. 28 ÷ 7 = 4

29. 14 ÷ 2 = 7

30. 50 ÷ 5 = 10

31. 9 ÷ 3 = 3

32. 48 ÷ 8 = 6

33. 36 ÷ 6 = 6

34. 63 ÷ 7 = ______

35. 42 ÷ 6 = ______

36. 35 ÷ 5 = 7

37. 18 ÷ 9 = 2

38. 81 ÷ 9 = 9

Division Fact Fun (continued)

Divide.

39. 10 ÷ 1 = ______

40. 6 ÷ 2 = ______

41. 27 ÷ 3 = ______

42. 28 ÷ 4 = ______

43. 25 ÷ 5 = ______

44. 54 ÷ 6 = ______

45. 14 ÷ 7 = ______

46. 64 ÷ 8 = ______

47. 81 ÷ 9 = ______

48. 3 ÷ 3 = ______

49. 6 ÷ 1 = ______

50. 18 ÷ 2 = ______

51. 30 ÷ 3 = ______

52. 12 ÷ 4 = ______

53. 35 ÷ 5 = ______

54. 48 ÷ 6 = ______

55. 72 ÷ 9 = ______

56. 90 ÷ 9 = ______

57. 2 ÷ 1 = ______

58. 15 ÷ 3 = ______

59. 42 ÷ 7 = ______

60. 27 ÷ 9 = ______

61. 10 ÷ 5 = ______

62. 36 ÷ 3 = ______

63. 8 ÷ 4 = ______

64. 12 ÷ 6 = ______

65. 72 ÷ 8 = ______

66. 1 ÷ 1 = ______

67. 10 ÷ 2 = ______

68. 45 ÷ 5 = ______

69. 35 ÷ 7 = ______

70. 18 ÷ 9 = ______

71. 5 ÷ 5 = ______

72. 2 ÷ 2 = ______

73. 24 ÷ 4 = ______

74. 56 ÷ 8 = ______

75. 7 ÷ 1 = ______

76. 20 ÷ 2 = ______

Divide Using Blocks

Pam wants to divide 86 cards among her 4 friends.
She uses blocks to model division. 86 = 8 tens and 6 ones

Pam shares out the tens and then the ones.
There are 2 tens and 1 one in each group. 2 ones are left.
So 86 ÷ 4 = 21 with 2 left over.

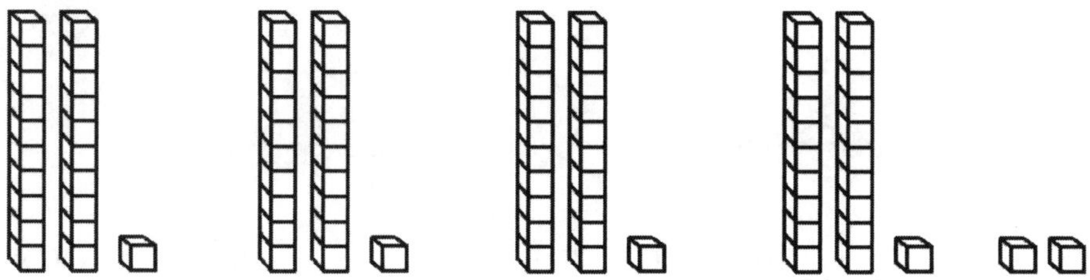

She uses long division to check.

$$\begin{array}{r} 21 \\ 4\overline{)86} \\ -\underline{8} \\ 6 \\ -\underline{4} \\ 2 \end{array}$$

- 4 groups → 4
- 21 ← 2 tens in each group, 1 one in each group
- 86 ← 86 cards
- 2 ← 2 ones left over

1. Use blocks to model division. Then divide.

$$\begin{array}{r} 24 \\ 2\overline{)48} \\ -\underline{4} \\ 8 \\ -\underline{8} \\ 2 \end{array}$$

<u>2</u> groups

<u>2 tens and 4 ones</u>
in each group

a) $3\overline{)75}$

_____ groups

____
in each group

b) $4\overline{)52}$

_____ groups

____
in each group

Divide Using Blocks (continued)

2. Divide. Write how many are left over.

a) $5\overline{)63}$

______ groups

_________ in each group

______ left over

b) $4\overline{)74}$

______ groups

_________ in each group

______ left over

c) $3\overline{)85}$

______ groups

_________ in each group

______ left over

d) $2\overline{)53}$

______ groups

_________ in each group

______ left over

e) $4\overline{)98}$

______ groups

_________ in each group

______ left over

f) $6\overline{)76}$

______ groups

_________ in each group

______ left over

3. Jenny plants 88 trees in 4 rows. How many trees are in each row? Use a model to help solve the problem.

Divide Two-Digit Numbers by One-Digit Numbers

2 tens in each group → 2 2 groups → $2\overline{)51}$ $-\ 4$ 11 **Step 1:** Divide to find how many tens can go in each group. **Step 2:** Multiply: 4 tens are placed. Subtract: 1 ten is left. So, 1 ten and 1 one are left. Write 1 beside the 1 ten.	25 ← 5 ones in each group $2\overline{)51}$ $-\ 4$ 11 $-\ 10$ 1 **Step 3:** Divide to find how many ones can go in each group. **Step 4:** Multiply to find 10 ones are placed. Subtract to find that 1 one is left. So, the answer is 25 R 1. R means remainder.

Find the quotient. Hint: The answer in division is called the **quotient**.

1. $3\overline{)53}$ **2.** $2\overline{)54}$ **3.** $2\overline{)35}$ **4.** $3\overline{)86}$

5. $4\overline{)92}$ **6.** $3\overline{)72}$ **7.** $2\overline{)79}$ **8.** $5\overline{)82}$

9. $4\overline{)98}$ **10.** $5\overline{)74}$ **11.** $6\overline{)89}$ **12.** $3\overline{)42}$

Divide Two-Digit Numbers by One-Digit Numbers (continued)

Divide. Hint: As you work, line up the tens and ones. Shade the tens column orange. Shade the ones column yellow.

13. $5\overline{)54}$

14. $6\overline{)76}$

15. $7\overline{)89}$

16. $4\overline{)90}$

17. $6\overline{)84}$

18. $8\overline{)98}$

19. $9\overline{)99}$

20. $6\overline{)86}$

21. $7\overline{)85}$

22. $8\overline{)89}$

23. $6\overline{)75}$

24. $5\overline{)73}$

Divide Multi-Digit Numbers

Divide.

```
      7 8
4 ) 3 1 2
  − 2 8
      3 2
    − 3 2
        0
```

Hint: There are fewer hundreds than groups. So, the division starts with the tens.

1. $2\overline{)5\,4\,3}$

2. $4\overline{)5\,3\,5}$

3. $3\overline{)8\,1\,6}$

4. $3\overline{)1\,9\,2}$

5. $4\overline{)7\,1\,2}$

6. $2\overline{)3\,7\,9}$

7. $6\overline{)8\,1\,2}$

8. $5\overline{)9\,1\,8}$

9. $4\overline{)3\,7\,4}$

10. $6\overline{)7\,4\,6}$

11. $3\overline{)4\,2\,3}$

Estimate a Quotient

Use **compatible numbers** to estimate a quotient.
Compatible numbers are numbers that divide evenly.

Estimate: 243 ÷ 6. Divide 6 into the first 2 digits. How many 6s are in 24?

Think: 24 ÷ 6 = 4
240 ÷ 6 = 40 Since it is an estimate, write 0 for the ones digit.
The estimated quotient is 40.

1. Use compatible numbers to estimate the quotient. Show your work.

a) $5\overline{)255}$

b) $6\overline{)246}$

c) $4\overline{)324}$

d) $7\overline{)491}$

e) $6\overline{)428}$

f) $3\overline{)128}$

Estimate a Quotient (continued)

Estimate: 312 ÷ 4
Think: About how many 4s are in 31?

28 ÷ 4 = 7 too small 32 ÷ 4 = 8 close 36 ÷ 4 = 9 too large

31 is close to 32.

32 ÷ 4 = 8 So, try 8.
320 ÷ 4 = 80 Write 0 for the ones digit.
The estimated quotient is 80.

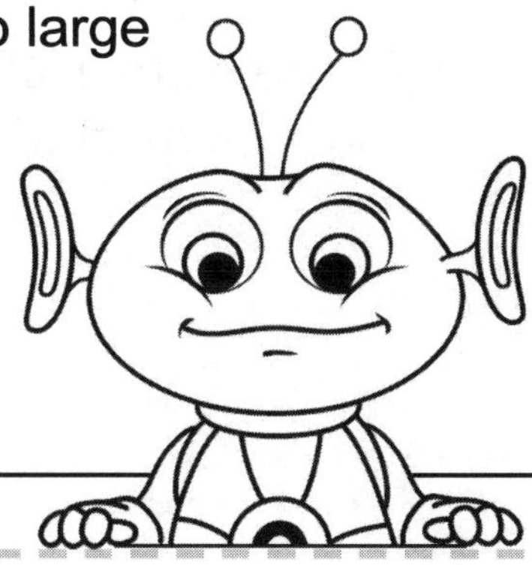

2. Estimate the quotient. Show your work.

a) $3\overline{)143}$

b) $4\overline{)254}$

c) $5\overline{)224}$

d) $5\overline{)365}$

e) $6\overline{)431}$

f) $8\overline{)634}$

Word Problems

Decide if you need to multiply or divide. Underline any words that help you decide. Circle Multiply or Divide. Then solve the problem. Show your work.

1. There were 132 students in 4 school buses. How many students were in each bus?

Multiply

Divide

2. Maylin biked an average of 32 kilometres each day for 9 days. How many kilometres did she bike in total?

Multiply

Divide

3. Damian has 75 tickets for rides at the amusement park. How many tickets will be left over if he shares the tickets equally among 7 friends?

Multiply

Divide

4. On average, Canadians use 329 litres of water per day. How much water does each Canadian use in a week?

Multiply

Divide

Add Decimal Numbers

You can use fraction strips to add decimals.
Shade the tenths in each number.

2.5 + 2.6 =

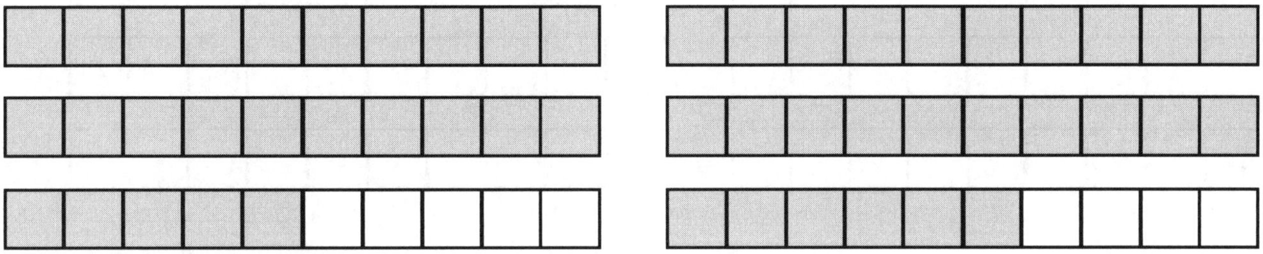

$\frac{5}{10}$ and $\frac{6}{10}$ = 1 whole and 1 tenth

Add the wholes and tenths: 2 + 2 + 1.1 = 5.1
So, 2.5 + 2.6 = *5.1*

1. Use fraction strips to for each number. Then add. Show your work.

a) 2.9 + 4.5 =

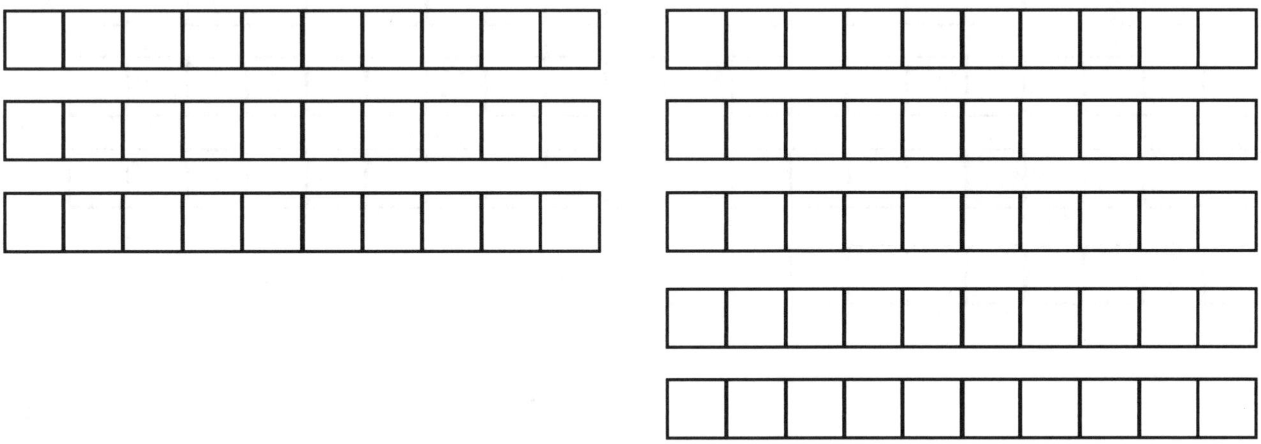

Add Decimal Numbers (continued)

b) 2.3 + 2.8 =

c) 2.8 + 3.7 =

d) 3.6 + 2.7 =

Subtract Decimal Numbers

You can use fraction strips to subtract decimals.
Shade the number of tenths in each number.

2.4 – 1.6 =

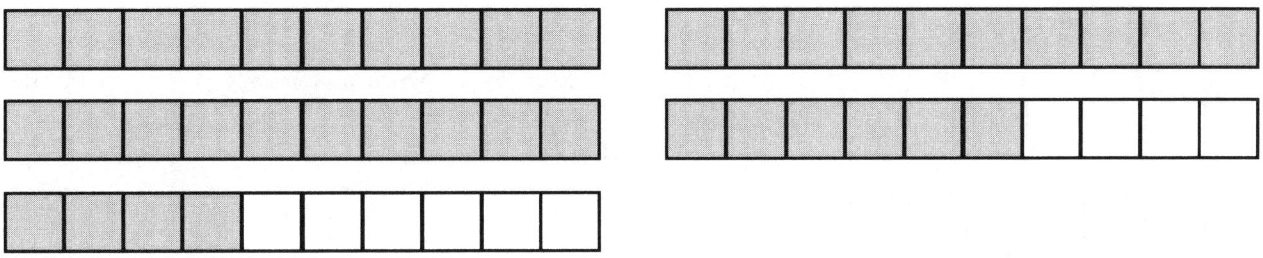

2.4 = ____ tenths and 1.6 = ____ tenths

2.4 – 1.6 = 24 tenths – 16 tenths

$= \frac{8}{10}$

2.4 – 1.6 = 0.8

1. Use fraction strips for each number. Then subtract.
Show your work.

a) 2.9 – 1.5 =

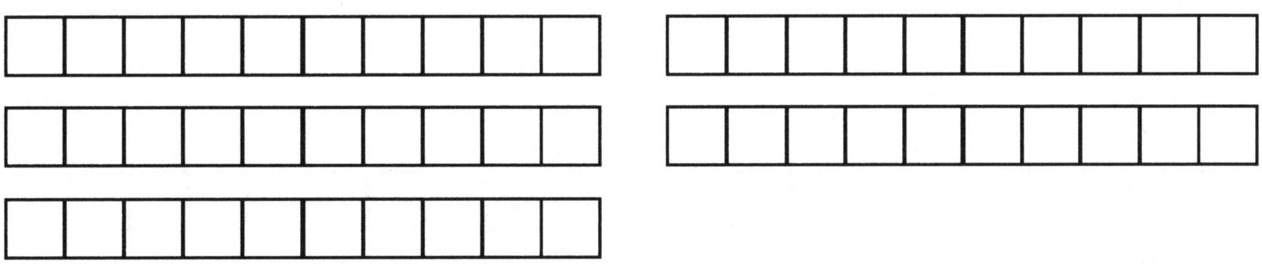

Subtract Decimal Numbers (continued)

b) 4.3 – 2.8 =

c) 3.5 – 1.7 =

d) 2.8 – 1.9 =

Comparing Fractions

Compare. Write < , >, or = .

1.
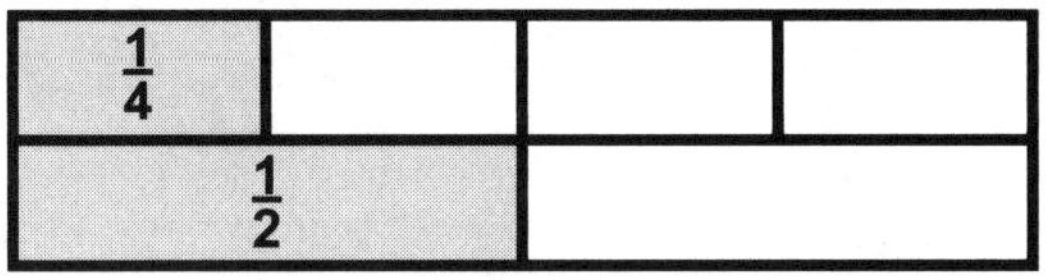

$\frac{1}{4}$ ☐ $\frac{1}{2}$

2.
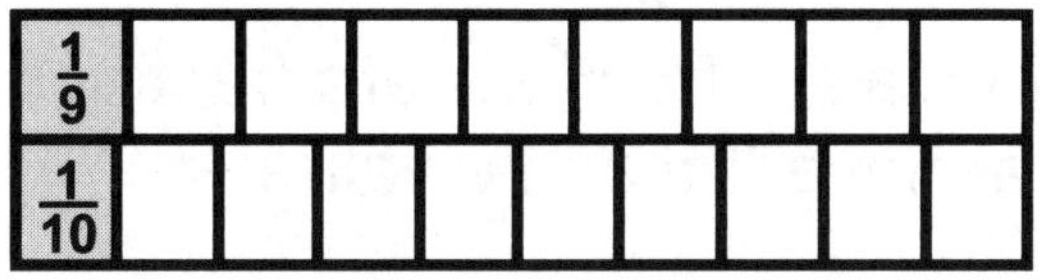

$\frac{1}{9}$ ☐ $\frac{1}{10}$

3.
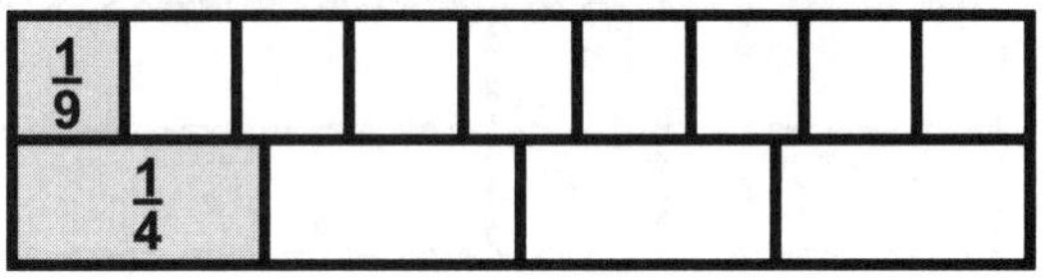

$\frac{1}{9}$ ☐ $\frac{1}{4}$

4.
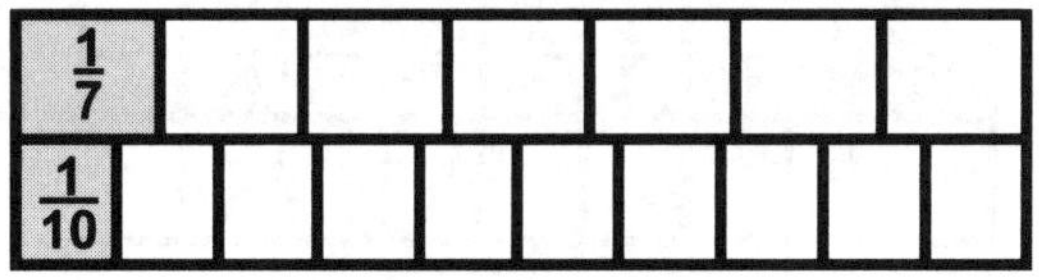

$\frac{1}{7}$ ☐ $\frac{1}{10}$

5.
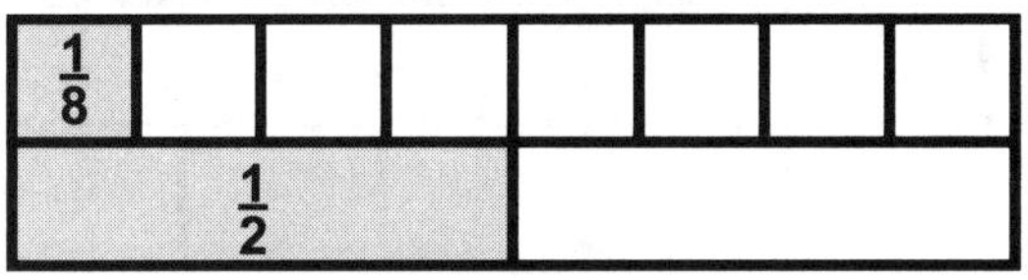

$\frac{1}{8}$ ☐ $\frac{1}{2}$

6.
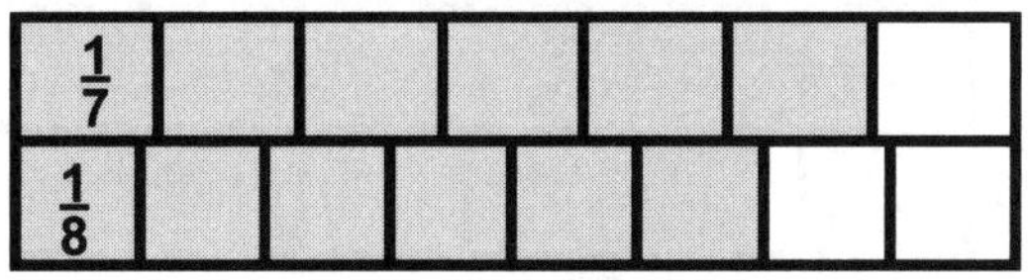

$\frac{6}{7}$ ☐ $\frac{6}{8}$

7.
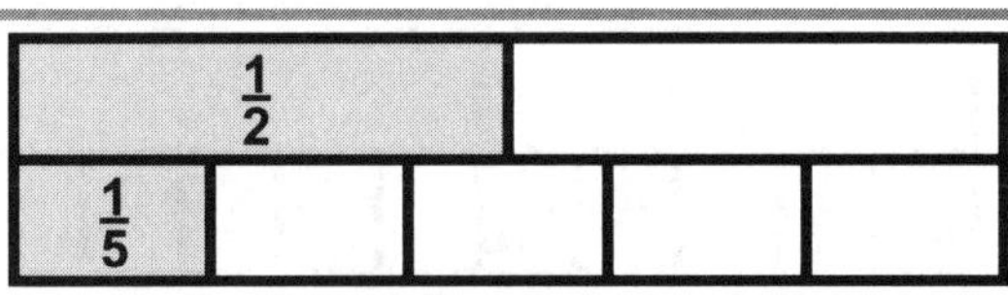

$\frac{1}{2}$ ☐ $\frac{1}{5}$

8.
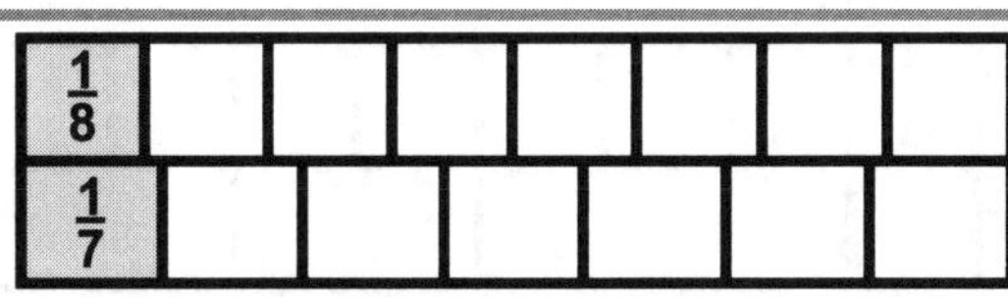

$\frac{1}{8}$ ☐ $\frac{1}{7}$

9.
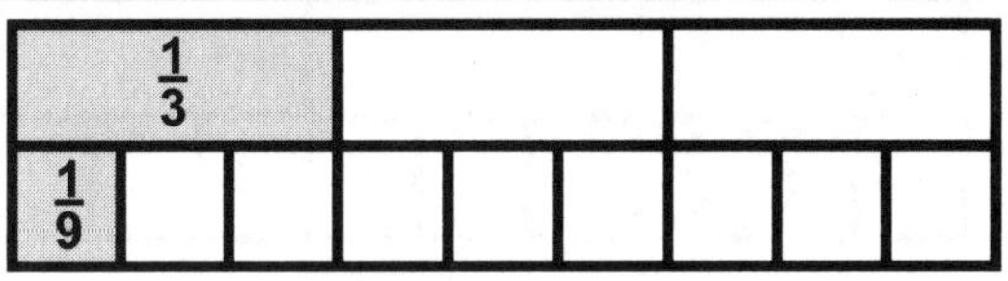

$\frac{1}{3}$ ☐ $\frac{1}{9}$

10.
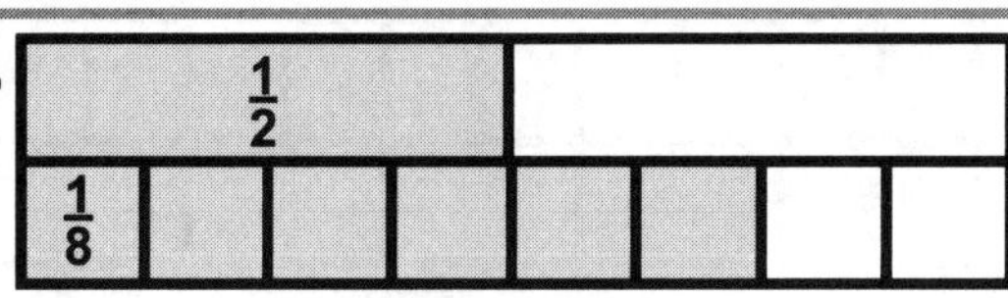

$\frac{1}{2}$ ☐ $\frac{6}{8}$

Equivalent Fractions

Fill in the missing number to make two equivalent fractions.

Equivalent fractions are fractions that have the same value.

1.

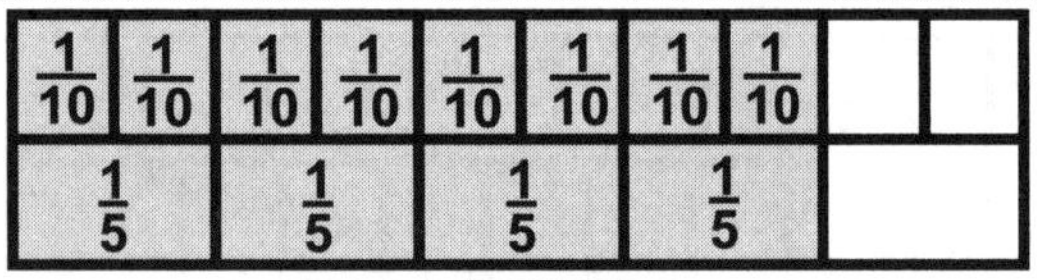

$\frac{8}{10} = \frac{\boxed{4}}{5}$

2.

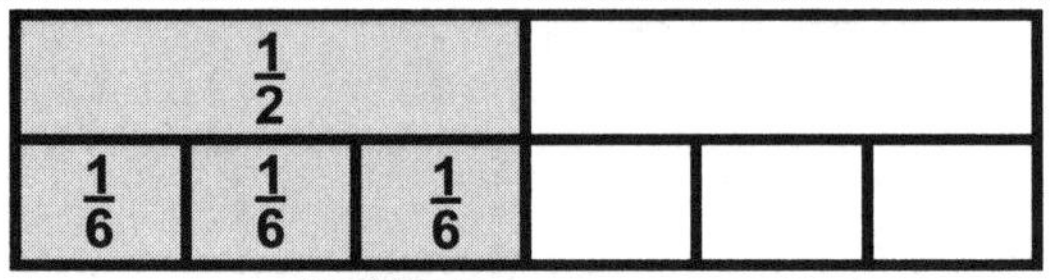

$\frac{\boxed{1}}{2} = \frac{3}{6}$

3.

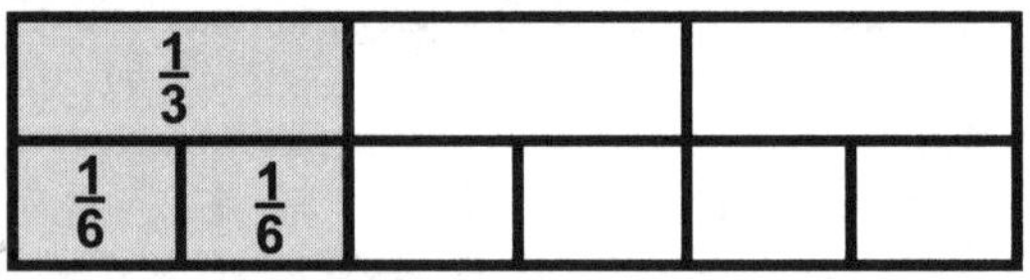

$\frac{\boxed{1}}{3} = \frac{2}{6}$

4.

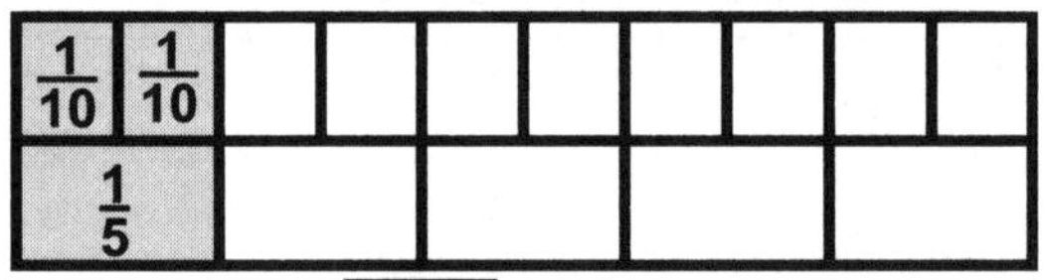

$\frac{\boxed{2}}{10} = \frac{1}{5}$

5.

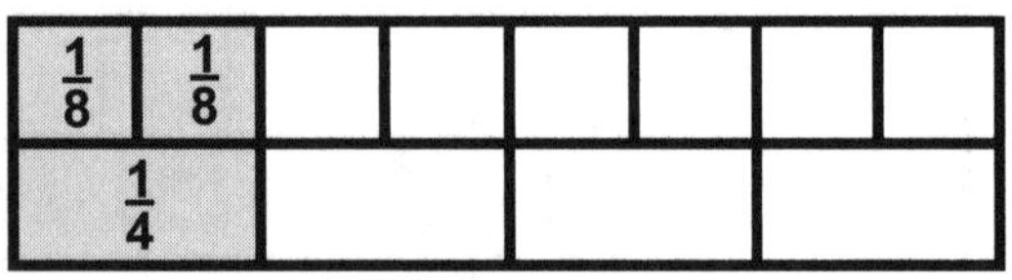

$\frac{\boxed{2}}{8} = \frac{1}{4}$

6.

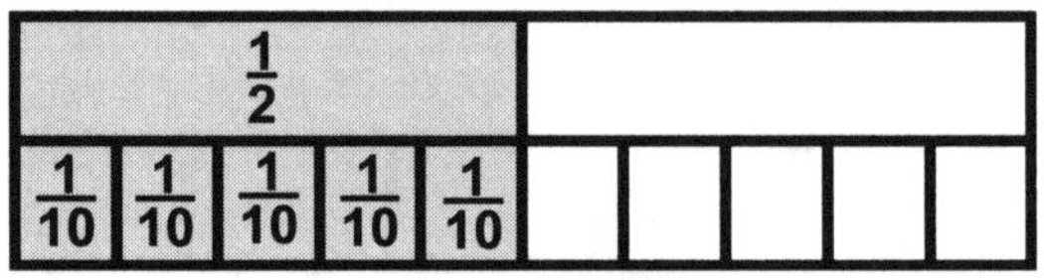

$\frac{1}{2} = \frac{\boxed{5}}{10}$

7.

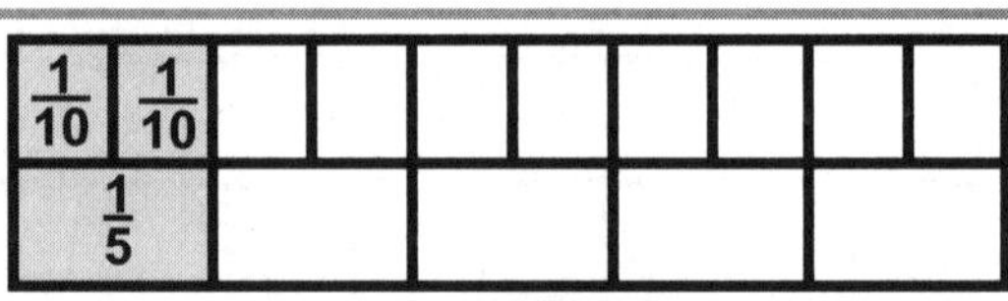

$\frac{2}{10} = \frac{\boxed{1}}{5}$

8.

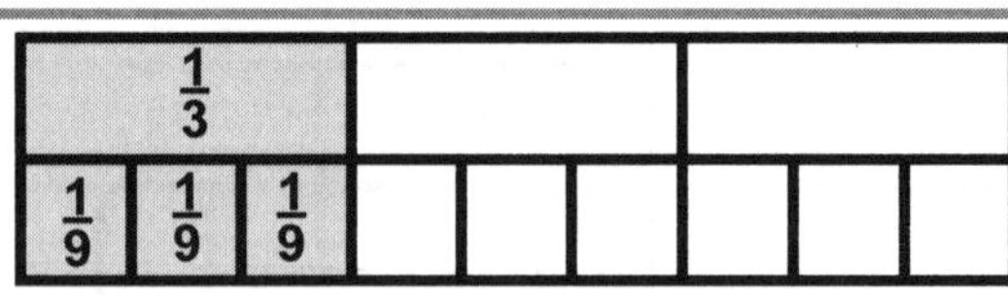

$\frac{1}{3} = \frac{\boxed{3}}{9}$

Adding Fractions

Add the fractions.

1. $\frac{3}{4} + \frac{1}{4} = \frac{4}{4}$	2. $\frac{1}{2} + \frac{1}{2} = \frac{2}{2}$	3. $\frac{1}{9} + \frac{5}{9} =$
4. $\frac{4}{7} + \frac{3}{7} =$	5. $\frac{2}{6} + \frac{4}{6} =$	6. $\frac{2}{5} + \frac{2}{5} =$
7. $\frac{1}{3} + \frac{1}{3} =$	8. $\frac{7}{8} + \frac{1}{8} =$	9. $\frac{4}{8} + \frac{2}{8} =$
10. $\frac{2}{4} + \frac{1}{4} =$	11. $\frac{4}{9} + \frac{5}{9} =$	12. $\frac{3}{5} + \frac{1}{5} =$
13. $\frac{1}{7} + \frac{2}{7} =$	14. $\frac{2}{3} + \frac{1}{3} =$	15. $\frac{1}{6} + \frac{5}{6} =$

BRAIN STRETCH

If you cut a cake into slices, circle which fraction shows the slice of cake that is the smallest.

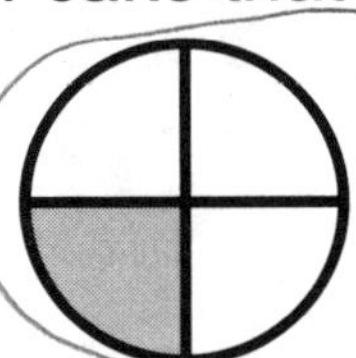
$\frac{1}{4}$

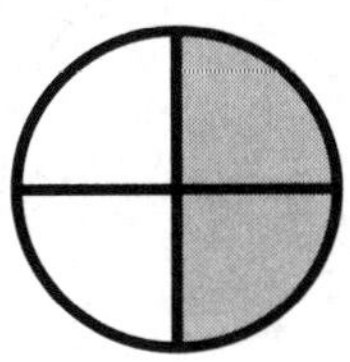
$\frac{1}{2}$

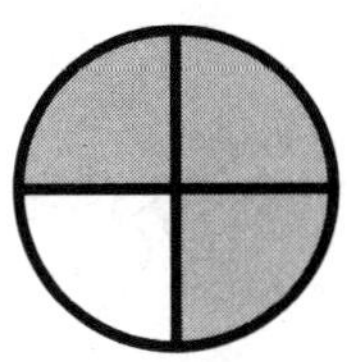
$\frac{3}{4}$

Subtracting Fractions

Subtract the fractions.

1. $\frac{4}{8} - \frac{2}{8} = \frac{2}{8}$
2. $\frac{2}{4} - \frac{1}{4} =$ ☐
3. $\frac{2}{3} - \frac{1}{3} =$ ☐
4. $\frac{6}{7} - \frac{1}{7} =$ ☐
5. $\frac{3}{4} - \frac{1}{4} =$ ☐
6. $\frac{4}{5} - \frac{1}{5} =$ ☐
7. $\frac{3}{6} - \frac{2}{6} =$ ☐
8. $\frac{5}{9} - \frac{3}{9} =$ ☐
9. $\frac{3}{7} - \frac{1}{7} =$ ☐
10. $\frac{4}{8} - \frac{3}{8} =$ ☐
11. $\frac{5}{9} - \frac{4}{9} =$ ☐
12. $\frac{3}{5} - \frac{1}{5} =$ ☐
13. $\frac{8}{9} - \frac{1}{9} =$ ☐
14. $\frac{4}{6} - \frac{2}{6} =$ ☐
15. $\frac{5}{7} - \frac{1}{7} =$ ☐

BRAIN STRETCH

If you circle $\frac{1}{2}$ of the creatures, how many creatures are left?

Exploring Decimal Fractions

A decimal is a way to write a fraction.

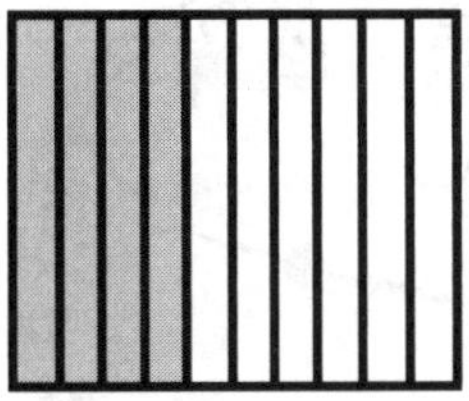

four tenths

$$\frac{4}{10} = 0.4$$

Read 0.4 as "four tenths."

The point means it is a decimal.

$$\frac{4}{100} = 0.04$$

Read 0.04 as "four hundredths."

Write each fraction as a decimal number. Colour the boxes that have tenths red. Colour the boxes that have hundredths green.

$\frac{8}{100} = \square$

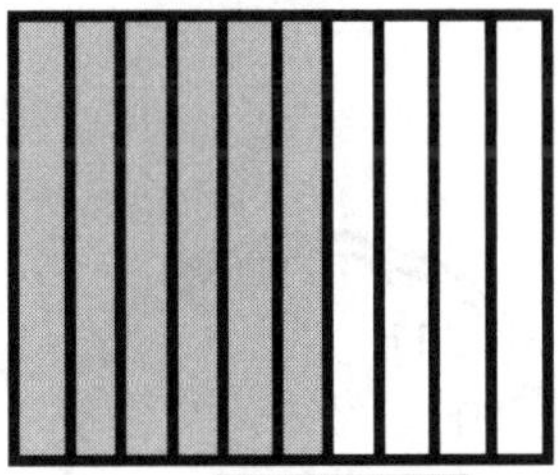

= $\square$

five hundredths

= $\square$

nine tenths

= $\square$

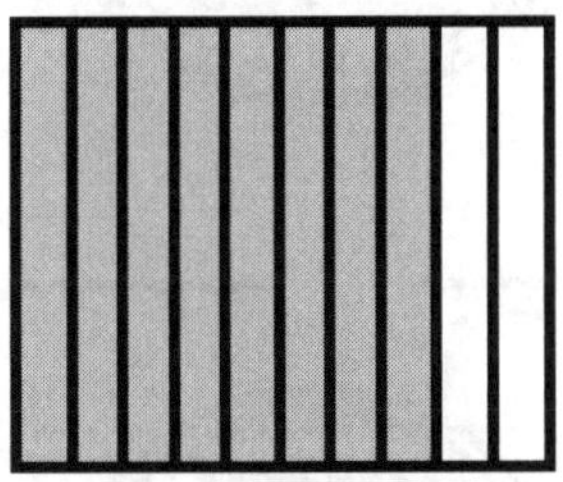

= $\square$

$\frac{76}{100} = \square$

$\frac{17}{100} = \square$

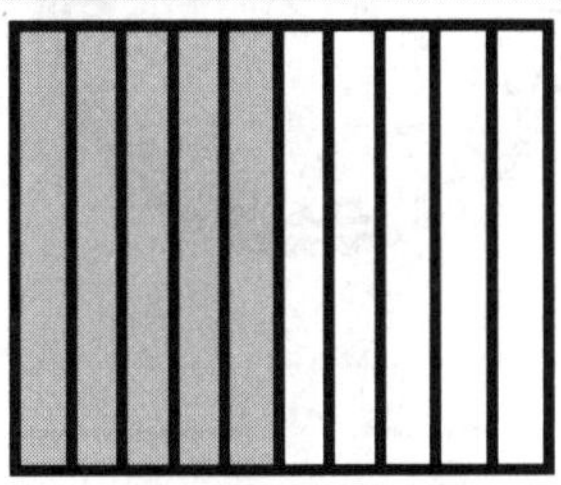

= $\square$

one tenth

= $\square$

What Time Is It?

A clock shows time using numbers and hands. The face of a clock shows the numbers 1 to 12. It takes 5 minutes for the long minute hand to move from one number to the next.

Each line on the face of the clock equals **1 minute**.

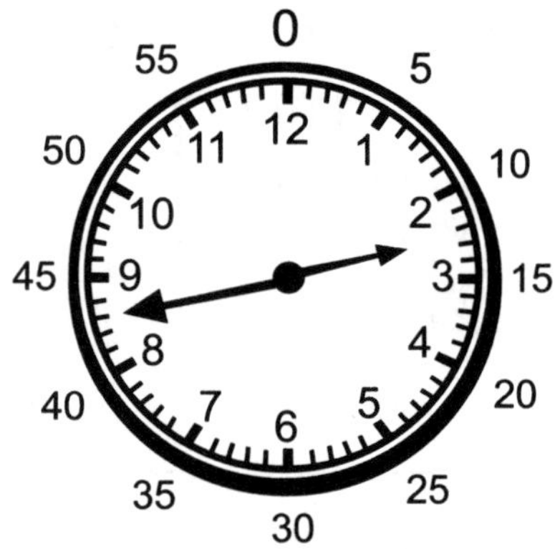

The time is 2:43.

Write the time to the nearest minute. Highlight the hour hand blue. Highlight the minute hand red.

1. 

_____ : _____

2. 

_____ : _____

3. 

_____ : _____

4. 

_____ : _____

5. 

_____ : _____

6. 

_____ : _____

Draw the Hands

Draw the two hands on the clock to show the time.
Highlight the hour hand blue. Highlight the minute hand red.

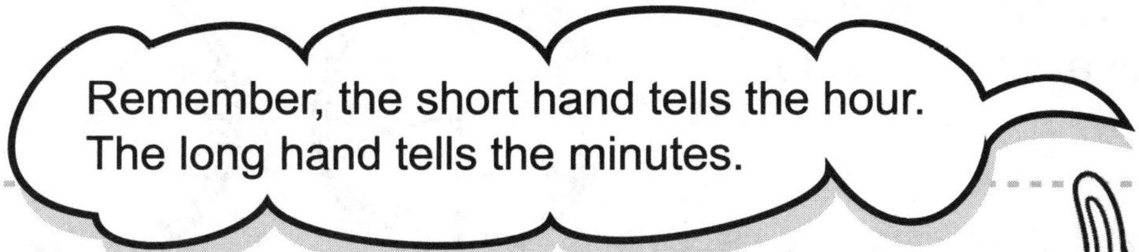

1. 

10:36

2. 

seven minutes after five

3. 

eighteen minutes to six

4. 

twenty-one minutes past three

5. 

sixteen minutes after one

6. 

6:28

7. 

three minutes after two

8. 

3:51

Elapsed Time

Elapsed time is the amount of time that has passed from the start of a time period to the end of a time period.

Start Time

End Time

1 hour and 25 minutes have elapsed.

Write the start time and the end time. Include the hours and minutes.

1. Start Time

______ : ______ p.m.

End Time

______ : ______ p.m.

What is the elapsed time?

____

2. Start Time

______ : ______ p.m.

End Time

______ : ______ p.m.

What is the elapsed time?

____

3. Start Time

______ : ______ p.m.

End Time

______ : ______ p.m.

What is the elapsed time?

____

Basketball Fun

1. Michael practices shooting baskets for 25 minutes each night. Fill in the chart below to show the start and end time of each night's practice.

a.m. refers to before midday   p.m. refers to after midday

Day of the Week	Start Time	Finish Time
Sunday	5:45 p.m.	
Monday		6:20 p.m.
Tuesday	5:35 p.m.	
Wednesday		7:25 p.m.
Thursday	5:40 p.m.	
Friday		4:55 p.m.
Saturday	5:05 p.m.	

2. How many minutes did Michael practice shooting basketballs for the whole week? ____________________

BRAIN STRETCH

Fill in the correct time. Be sure to include a.m. or p.m.

a) This morning, Sophia woke up at:

_____ : _____ ☐

b) Sophia did her homework after school for 1 hour and 25 minutes. She finished at the time on the clock. When did she start?

_____ : _____ ☐

Solve Problems About Time

Ben wakes up at 7:00 a.m. It takes him 5 minutes to shower, 5 minutes to dress, 10 minutes to make lunch, 15 minutes to eat breakfast, and 5 minutes to brush his teeth. How many minutes does he have until the bus comes at 8:00?

Draw arrows to show how the minute hand moved each time.

Count by 5s to find out how much time has gone by.

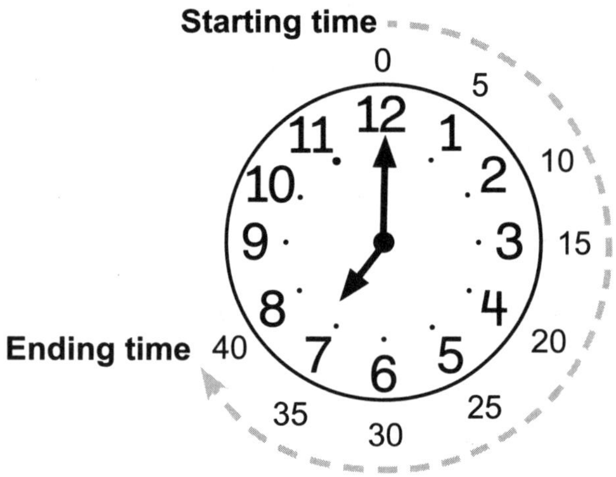

It takes Ben 40 minutes to get ready.
From 7:40 to 8:00, there are 20 minutes.
Ben has 20 minutes to spare.

Use a time line to help.

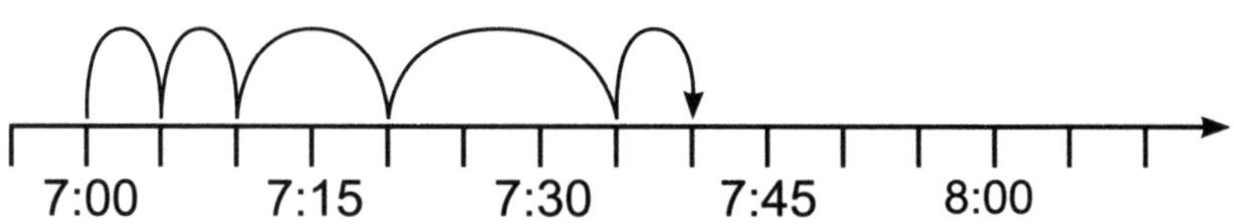

1. Cam gets up at 7:15. It takes her 10 minutes to shower, 10 minutes to dress, 20 minutes to eat breakfast, 10 minutes to brush her teeth, 5 minutes to get her backpack ready, and 15 minutes to walk to school. What time will she arrive at school?

a) Estimate. _______________

b) Solve the problem. Show your work using the time line.

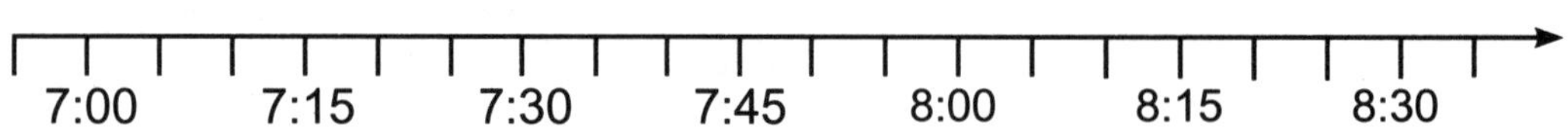

Solve Problems About Time (continued)

2. Write a list of tasks you do before school and the time it takes to do each one. Make up your own problem about time. Use the time line to show your work.

Tasks:

Jason started jogging at 2:10. He jogged for 45 minutes.
At what time did he stop jogging?

2:10	start time
+ 0:45	stop time
2:55	

Jason stopped jogging at 2:55.

3. Find the stop time by adding.

a)	**b)**	**c)**	**d)**
2:45	4:15	5:25	6:30
+ 0:10	+ 0:35	+ 1:00	+ 0:29
______	______	______	______

4. Melanie started playing piano at 3:15. She played for 30 minutes. At what time did she stop playing?

5. Add to find the stop time. Hint: 60 minutes = 1 hour. An example is done for you.

```
  7:10
+ 0:50
------
  7:60   60 minutes = 1 h
------
  7:60  is the same as 8:00
```

a)	b)	c)	d)
1:25	4:10	10:45	8:20
+ 0:35	+ 2:55	+ 1:40	+ 3:55
______	______	______	______
same as ______	same as ______	same as ______	same as ______

6. Adam started playing hockey at 4:30. He played for 1 hour and 30 minutes. At what time did he stop playing?

MONDAY Patterning and Algebra

1. 19 – 5 = _____

2. 20 + _____ = 27

3. Extend the following pattern.

   3, 6, 9, 12, _____, _____, _____

4. Is this a growing, shrinking or repeating pattern?

   30, 27, 24, 21, 18

5. Create a pattern based on the following rule: start at 10, add 5

TUESDAY Number Sense

1. Elizabeth is 7th in line to get a drink after gym. How many people are in front of her?

   ____

2. Order these numbers from least to greatest.

   8791, 7918, 7911

   ________, ________, ________

3. What is the greatest number you can make from these digits?

   3 6 1 5 ______________

4. Round these numbers to the nearest ten.

   456 ________ 284 ________

5. Multiply: 3 × 5 =

WEDNESDAY Geometry and Spatial Sense

1. Name this shape.

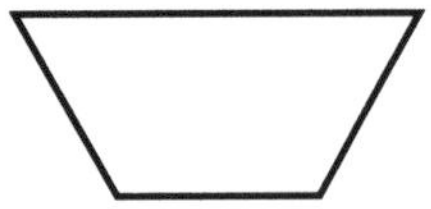

____

2. How many sides does a polygon have?

3. Name this 3D figure.

____

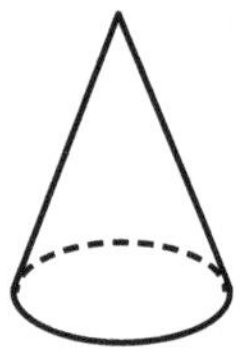

4. Look at the shapes. Choose flip, slide or turn.

A. flip B. slide C. turn

5. What is a quadrilateral?

____

THURSDAY Measurement

1. How many mm in one cm?

____

2. What time is it?

____

3. Should you measure a pencil with m, cm or km?

____

4. What does km stand for?

____

5. Perimeter = ________ units

Area = ________ square units

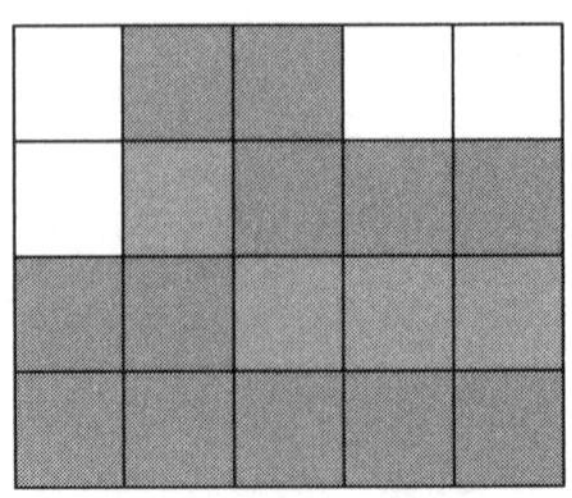

FRIDAY Data Management

The grade four classes took a survey of their favourite sports. They displayed the data as a pictograph. Use their pictograph to answer the questions.

Soccer	☺☺☺☺
Basketball	☺☺☺☺☺☺☺☺
Hockey	☺☺☺☺☺☺☺☺☺

☺ = 2 students

1. How many students took part in the survey? ____________

2. What was the most popular sport? ____________________

3. How many more students preferred hockey over basketball?

____

4. List the favourite sports from least to greatest.

____

5. What would be a good title for this pictograph?

____

BRAIN STRETCH

1. How many weeks are there in one year? ________________

2. How many weeks are there in two years? ________________

3. How many weeks are there in five years? ________________

MONDAY Patterning and Algebra

1. ___ + 5 = 20

2. Complete the following pattern:

   5, 10, 15, 20, _____, _____, _____

3. Complete the following pattern:

   11, 22, 11, 22, _____, _____, _____

4. Complete the following pattern:

   80, 70, 60, 50, _____, _____, _____

5. Divide:

   $72 \div 8 =$

TUESDAY Number Sense

1. Write the numeral.

   twelve thousand two hundred five

2. Order these numbers from least to greatest.

   4723, 7432, 7324

   _______, _______, _______

3. What is the greatest number you can make from these digits?

   1 6 4 5 __________

4. Round these numbers to the nearest hundred:

   1263 ______ 2730 ______

5. What is the value of the money?

WEDNESDAY Geometry and Spatial Sense

1. Name this shape.

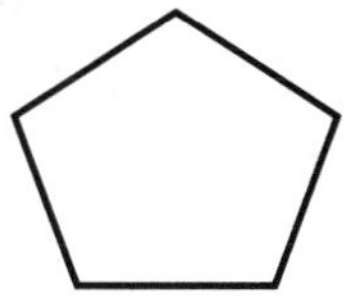

____

2. How many parallel sides does a square have?

3. Name this 3D figure.

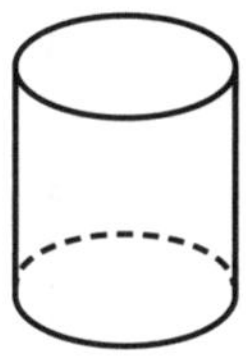

____

4. Look at the shapes. Choose flip, slide or turn.

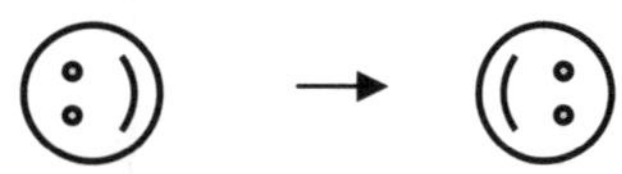

A. flip   B. slide   C. turn

5. Name a quadrilateral.

____

THURSDAY Measurement

1. How many m in a km?

2. What temperature is it most likely if you are in a bathing suit at the beach?

A. 30°C   B. - 3°C   C. 6°C

3. How long would it take to write the date on a piece of paper?

A. 1 min   B. 1 day   C. 1 hour

4. What time is it?

____

5. Would you measure the height of a house with m, cm or mm?

FRIDAY Data Management

Sarah's music class took a survey of studnets in her school to see what kind of music they preferred. Here are her results: 12 preferred reggae, 2 classical, 28 dance music, 17 rock 'n' roll, and 14 preferred country.

Reggae	Classical	Dance	Rock 'n' Roll	Country

1. Use the table above to show a tally of the results.

2. What was the most popular style of music? ______________________

3. What was the least popular style of music? ______________________

4. How many more students preferred dance music to country music?

____

5. How many students participated in this survey? ______________________

BRAIN STRETCH

John has 1268 marbles and wants to give his sister half of them.
How many will he give her?

MONDAY Patterning and Algebra

1. 50 – 25 =

2. What kind of pattern is this?

   12, 24, 36, 48

   A. growing B. repeating C. shrinking

3. 12 + 10 =

4. 20 - ____= 12

5. Continue the pattern:

   11, 22, 33, 44, _____, _____, _____

TUESDAY Number Sense

1. What number is 1000 more than 7983?

2. How many thousands in 5746?

3. Multiply:

   65 X 10 =

4. Write the numeral for:

   eight hundred sixteen

5. What is the value of the money?

WEDNESDAY Geometry and Spatial Sense

1. Name this shape.

____

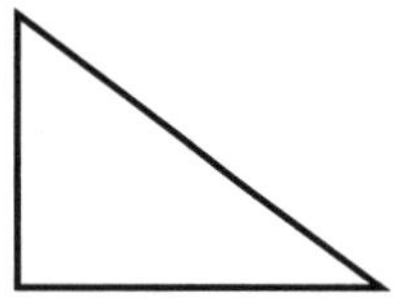

2. How many parallel sides does a diamond have?

____

3. Name this 3D figure.

____

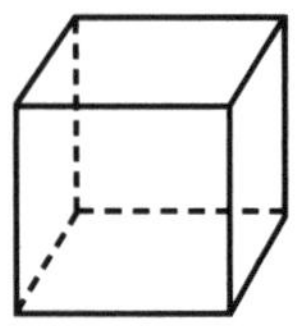

4. What shape is not a quadrilateral?

A. octagon

B. rhombus

C. square

5. How many sides and vertices does an octagon have?

sides __________ vertices __________

THURSDAY Measurement

1. 1 m = ____cm

2. 2 dm = __cm

3. What unit of measurement would you use to measure the distance from your house to school?

4. What time is it?

5. What is the area covered?

_____ square units

FRIDAY Data Management

Ms. Jenkins wanted to make a community quilt and asked her neighbours what their favourite colours were so that she could include them in her design. She made a graph from the data she collected.

Title______________________________________

Favourite Colour

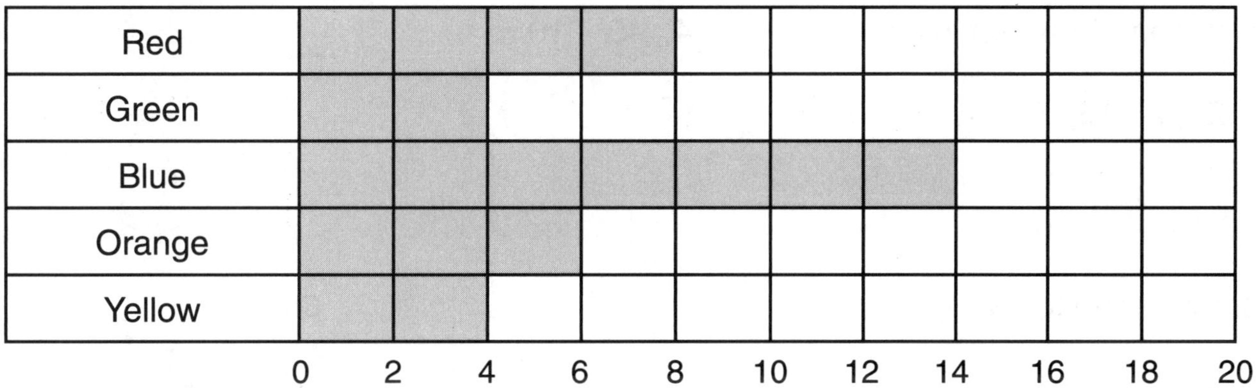

1. Label the graph.

2. What is the most favourite colour? ________________________

3. Which two colours are least favourite? _____________________

4. How many people were asked in this survey?________________

BRAIN STRETCH

If you had to build a tower with only one type of 3D figure, what 3D figure would you use? Why?

MONDAY Patterning and Algebra

1. What kind of pattern is it?

   2, 4, 6, 8, 10,12, 14

2. What kind of pattern is it?

   2, 2, 2, 3, 3, 3, 4, 4, 4, 5, 5, 5

3. What kind of pattern is it?

   24, 22, 20,18,16

4. 45 – 10 =

5. Complete the following:

   12 + ___ = 23

TUESDAY Number Sense

1. Order these numbers from least to greatest.

   2745, 2543, 3245

   _______, _______, ________

2. Order these numbers from least to greatest.

   5208, 8052, 5028

   _______, _______, ________

3. Subtract:

$$\begin{array}{r} 6605 \\ -\ 3252 \\ \hline \end{array}$$

4. Multiply:

$$\begin{array}{r} 45 \\ \times\ 4 \\ \hline \end{array}$$

5. What is the greatest number you can make from these digits:

   8 6 1 2

WEDNESDAY Geometry and Spatial Sense

1. Name this shape.

____

2. What is the name of a polygon with eight sides?

____

3. How many lines of symmetry?

K ________

4. How many vertices does a triangle have?

____

5. What is the name of this 3D figure?

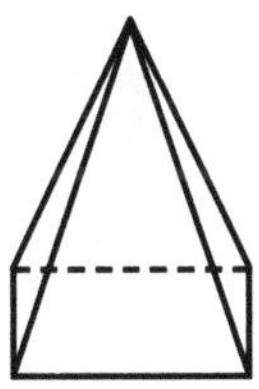

____

THURSDAY Measurement

1. 6 cm = ______ mm

2. 7000 mm = _______m

3. What unit of measure would you use to measure the width of your finger?

4. It is 7:50 am. What time will it be in 40 minutes?

5. Find the perimeter and area of the rectangle.

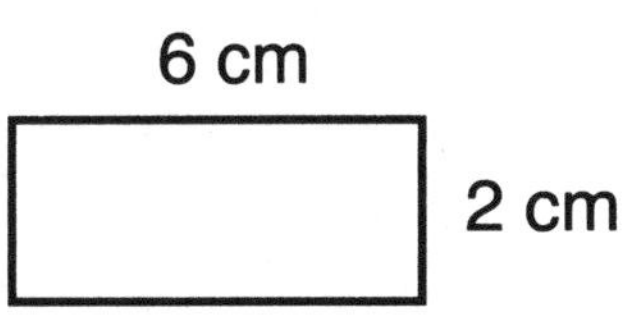

P = ____________

A = ____________

FRIDAY Data Management

The graph below shows the average yearly precipitation in seven different towns

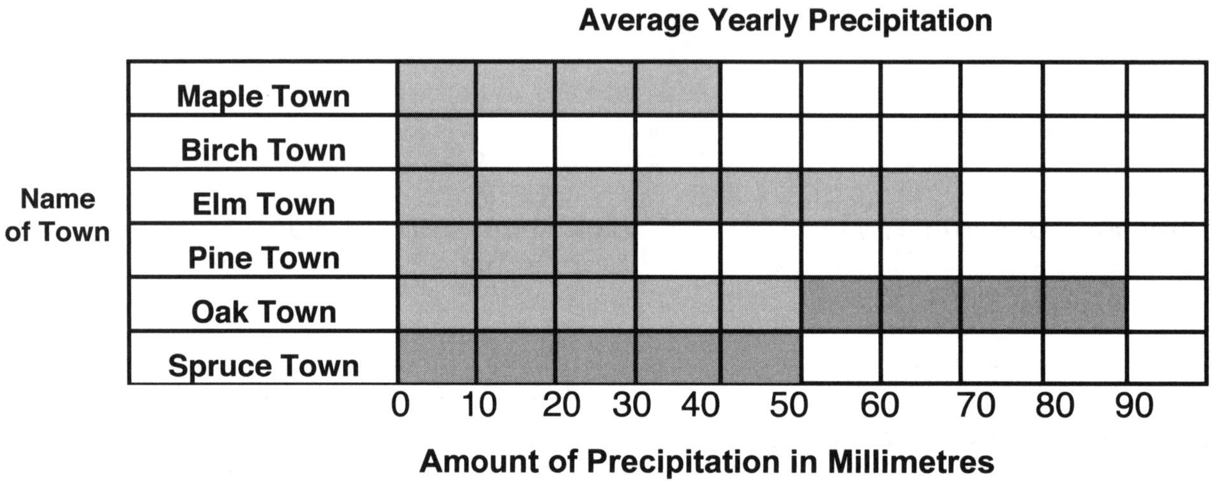

1. Which city had the most precipitation? ____________________

2. Which city had the least precipitation? ____________________

3. What is the range of the data shown? ____________________

4. How much more precipitation did Oak Town have than Pine Town?

____

5. List the towns in order from least precipitation to the most precipitation.

____

BRAIN STRETCH

What is the perimeter of a rectangular field that is 3 m by 4 m? What is the perimeter in cm?

MONDAY Patterning and Algebra

1. Create a pattern based on the following rule:

   start at 2, add 2

2. Create a pattern based on the following rule:

   start at 1, add 5

3. Create a pattern based on the following rule:

   start at 20, subtract 2

4. Create a pattern based on the following rule:

   start at 3, add 3

5. What is the number that completes the following equation?

   $7 + 9 = 8 + \_\_\_\_$

TUESDAY Number Sense

1. Add:

   $$\begin{array}{r} 5778 \\ +\ 3641 \\ \hline \end{array}$$

2. Round to the nearest ten.

   5281

3. What number is 1000 more than 4821?

   ____

4. Choose: >, <, or =.

   128 ☐ 128

5. Make the greatest possible number with these digits:

   7 3 1 4

WEDNESDAY Geometry and Spatial Sense

1. Name this shape.

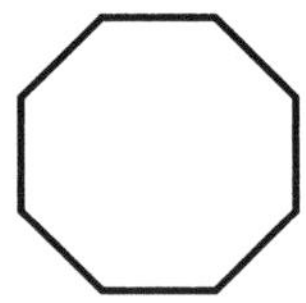

____

2. What is the name of a polygon with five sides?

____

3. How many lines of symmetry?

V _______

4. How many vertices does a pentagon have?

____

5. What is the name of this 3D figure?

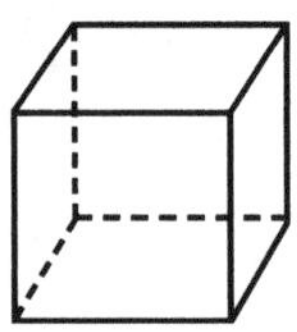

____

THURSDAY Measurement

1. How many decades in 3 centuries?

2. Find the perimeter of a square that has 12 m sides.

3. 900 mm = ____ dm

4. What time is it?

5. Mary wants to build a fence around her rectangular garden. It is 10 m wide and 15 m long. How much fencing does she need to buy?

FRIDAY Data Management

Sam and Shawn surveyed the traffic that passed by their apartment building during the lunch hour. They collected their data using the tally below.

Type of Vehicle	Tally	Number
Cars	𝍸 𝍸 |	
Trucks	||||	
Vans	𝍸 𝍸 |||	
Buses	𝍸 𝍸 𝍸 𝍸 ||	

1. How many vehicles passed their building? ____________

2. Which was the most common vehicle? ____________

3. How many more vans than cars passed them? ____________

4. How many fewer trucks than buses passed them? ____________

5. How many more buses than trucks passed them? ________________

BRAIN STRETCH

Mr. Turnbull's class raised $3100 to buy new computers. If a computer costs $800, how many computers can they buy?

MONDAY Patterning and Algebra

1. Create a pattern based on the following rule:

   start at 30, add 5

2. Create a pattern based on the following rule:

   start at 100, subtract 20

3. What is the missing number?

   81 ÷ ☐ = 9

4. What is the pattern rule?

   8, 16, 32, 64

5. What is the number that completes the following equation?

   14 - 8 = 13 - ____

TUESDAY Number Sense

1. Estimate the sum:

   244 + 122

2. Estimate the sum:

   899 + 501

3. Add:

   124 + 355

4. Add:

   456 +331

5. 147 students attended the fair in the day and 234 students attended at night. How many students attended in total?

WEDNESDAY Geometry and Spatial Sense

1. What is a vertex?

2. How many sides does a parallelogram have?

3. Draw the lines of symmetry for this square.

4. What 3D figure does this object look like?

5. Draw the reflection of this shape:

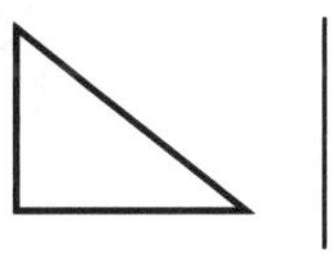

THURSDAY Measurement

1. Draw a rectangle with an area of 24 units^2.

2. What is the area of this shape?

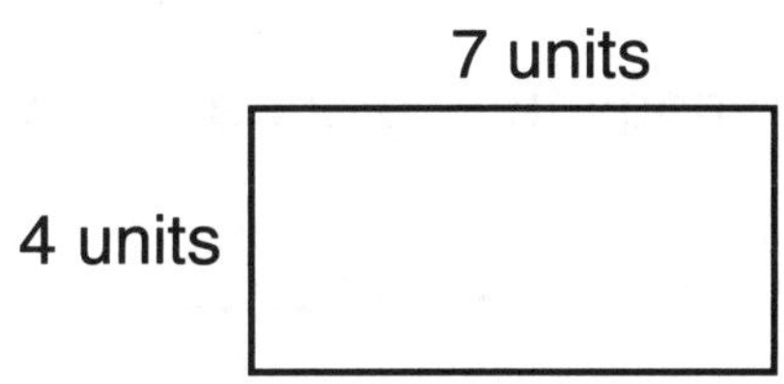

3. Draw rectangle with a perimeter of 12 units.

4. What time is it?

5. How many minutes in 4 hours?

FRIDAY Data Management

During the Annual Community Pet Show, Martha surveyed the contestants. Use the space below to create a bar graph of Martha's data. Here are her results:

30 cats **22 dogs** **5 ferrets** **10 parrots** **8 guinea pigs**

1. What was the most popular pet? ___________

2. How many pets came to the show? ____________

3. How many more dogs than guinea pigs were there? _________

4. What is the range of her data? ______________

BRAIN STRETCH

Marlene's mom lets her play video games for 30 minutes every night. How many hours does she play in a week? How many hours does she play in a month?

MONDAY Patterning and Algebra

1. Complete the following equation:

   12 + 10 = 15 + ___

2. Complete the following equation:

   5 + 2 = 6 + ___

3. Complete the following equation:

   25 – 6 = ___ - 11

4. Complete the following equation:

   89 = 21 + ____

5. Create a repeating pattern.

TUESDAY Number Sense

1. Estimate the difference:

   100 - 21

2. Estimate the difference:

   405 - 220

3. Subtract:

   346 - 232

4. Subtract:

   568 - 447

5. Sheila had $90. She bought two books for $18 each.
   How much money does she have left over?

WEDNESDAY Geometry and Spatial Sense

1. Draw a parallelogram.

2. How many more sides does an octagon have than a triangle?

3. Can a cube roll?

4. Circle the quadrilaterals.

4. What shape is the face of a cone?

THURSDAY Measurement

1. Name an object shorter than a decimetre.

2. 8 m = ________mm

3. What unit of measure would you use to measure a drop of rain?

4. It is 2:35 pm. What time will it be in 45 minutes?

5. Find the perimeter and area of the rectangle.

9 cm

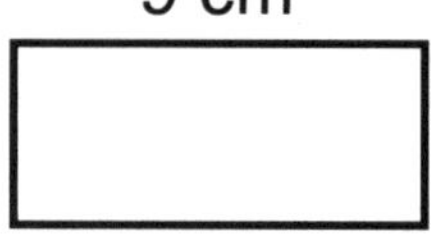

7 cm

P = ______________

A = ______________

FRIDAY Data Management

Sam had 10 marbles in a bag: 3 brown and 7 yellow.

1. How likely is it that he will choose a brown marble?

2. How likely is it that Sam will choose a yellow marble?

3. What is the probability of choosing a brown marble?

4. What is the probability of choosing a yellow marble?

5. How likely is it that you will watch television today?

BRAIN STRETCH

The Northland Science Reserve has many fields in which their animals can feed and play. Small farm animals have a field measuring 15 m by 10 m.

1. What is the perimeter of the field?

2. What is the area of the field?

3. If it costs $10 for each metre of fencing, how much will it cost to buy a new fence for the field?

MONDAY Patterning and Algebra

1. Use the rule to make a pattern:

   start at 4, multiply by 4

2. Use the rule to make a pattern:

   start at 2, multiply by 3

3. What is the missing number?

   $\square \div 7 = 7$

4. What is the pattern rule?

   99, 88, 77, 66

5. Create a growing pattern.

TUESDAY Number Sense

1. Add:

   5672 + 367

2. Add:

   599 + 405 =

3. Subtract:

   74 - 34

4. Subtract:

   68 - 49

5. Mrs. Stevens' class used 188 notebooks from a box of 250.
   How many were left?

WEDNESDAY Geometry and Spatial Sense

1. A square does not have right angles.

   true or false

2. Which of the following 3D figures does not roll?

   A. cylinder B. cone C. cube

3. How many edges does a pyramid have?

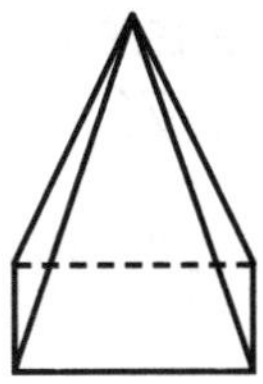

4. Draw a net for a cube.

5. Circle the following pairs of lines that intersect.

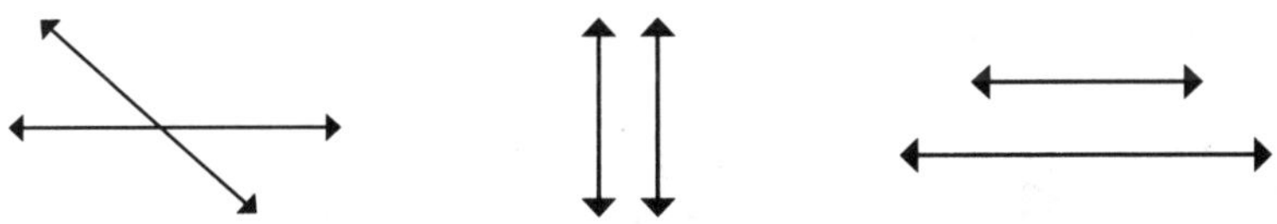

THURSDAY Measurement

1. What is the perimeter of a pentagon with sides each 4 cm long?

2. 2 km = _____cm

3. What is longer?

   A. 100 cm B. 10 m C. 1 km

4. How many years in 3 centuries?

5. What is the area covered?

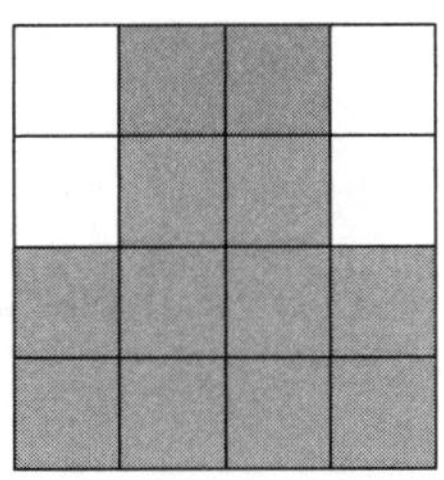

FRIDAY Data Management

1. When rolling a die, what is the probability that you will roll a 2?

2. What is the probability of rolling a 3?

3. What is the probability of rolling an even number? An odd number?

4. What is the probability of rolling a 7?

5. What is the value of the tally marks?

BRAIN STRETCH

A jar can hold 500 ml of jam.

1. Express that amount in litres.

2. How many jars will you need to have 6.5 L of jam?

3. How much will the jam in question 2 cost if each jar is $2.00?

MONDAY Patterning and Algebra

1. Complete the pattern:

   1, 3, 9, 27, ______, ______, ______

2. Complete the pattern:

   4, 8,12,16, ______, ______, ______

3. Complete the pattern:

   6,12,18, ______, ______, ______

4. Complete the pattern:

   20, 18, 16, 14, ______, ______, ______

5. Create a shrinking pattern.

TUESDAY Number Sense

1. Name the factors for 24.

2. Divide:

   $9\overline{)21}$

3. Write 45 023 in expanded form.

4. What number is 1000 less than 3512?

5. Write the following in standard form:

   2000 + 400 + 60 + 5

WEDNESDAY Geometry and Spatial Sense

1. Classify the following pair of lines.

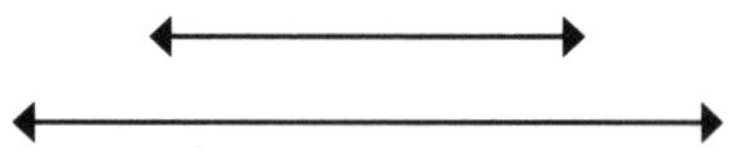

A. intersecting B. parallel C. perpendicular

2. Classify this triangle.

3. An angle of 150° is called?

A. obtuse B. right C. acute

4. Classify this angle.

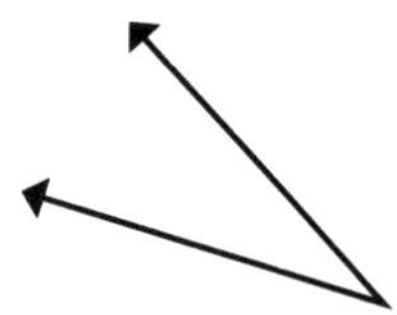

5. Name a 3D figure that does not have edges.

THURSDAY Measurement

1. 200 mm = ___dm

2. 16 km =______m

3. Find the perimeter of the figure:

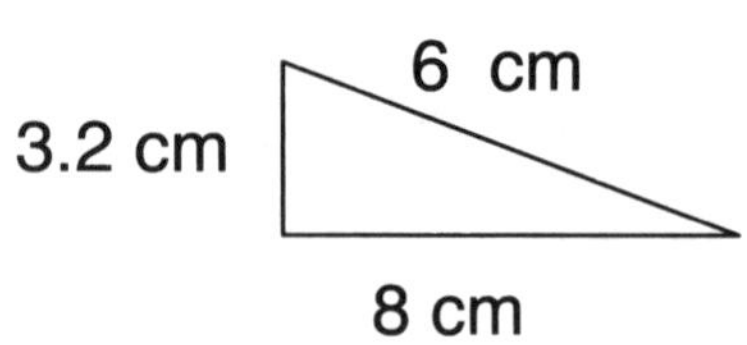

4. How many decades in 3 centuries?

5. Find the area of a square that has 3 m sides.

FRIDAY Data Management

Mr. Ramesh created a graph showing how he and his family spent their holiday.

1. What kind of graph did he create?

2. Where did they spend most of their vacation?

3. What sorts of activities did the Ramesh family do on their vacations?

4. What did they do the least amount of time?

5. Where do you think they might have gone on their holiday?

BRAIN STRETCH

Rick is older than John. John is older than Betty. Betty is older than Tina, and Vivienne is older than Rick. Who the oldest?

MONDAY Patterning and Algebra

1. Are the sums in each pair equal?

   2 + 6 1 + 7

2. Complete.

   16 - 7 = 18 - ______

3. Write 10 as the sum of 3 numbers.

4. Predict what the 21st figure will be in this pattern.

A.  B.  C. 

5. If each bag holds 15 jelly beans. How many jelly beans will there be in 6 bags?

TUESDAY Number Sense

1. Which digit is in the hundreds place?

   4955

2. Use the digits 8,9,3,2 to create the greatest number possible.

3. Subtract:

   7830
   - 6782

4. Order these numbers from greatest to least.

   1751, 7450, 4531, 4879

   ______, ______, ______, ______

5. What is the value of the money?

WEDNESDAY Geometry and Spatial Sense

1. How many lines of symmetry?

   G

2. What is the name of this shape?

3. How many vertices does this shape have?

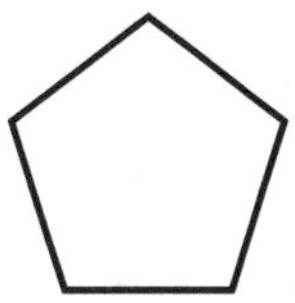

4. What 3D figure could be made from these pieces?

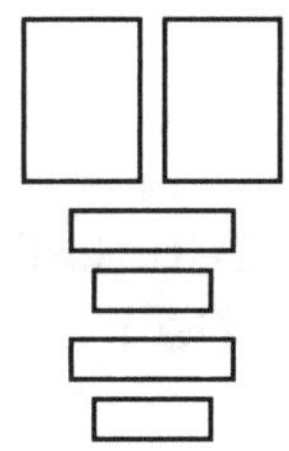

   A. cylinder
   B. rectangular prism
   C. pyramid

5. Name a type of triangle.

THURSDAY Measurement

1. What time is it?

2. Kate and Mark went for a 6 km hike. How many metres did they hike?

3. Find the perimeter of the octagon.

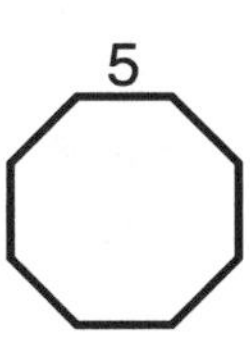

4. What is the year 1 decade after 1974?

5. 3000 m = ________km

FRIDAY Data Management

Darcy celebrated her ninth birthday at a local fairground. She invited her seven closest friends. She took a survey of their heights to see which rides they could go on. Here are her results:

Samantha 124 cm
Martin 146 cm
Darcy 130 cm
Larissa 129 cm
Josie 109 cm
Martha 140 cm
Jon 122 cm
Michael 145 cm

1. There is a 120 cm height requirement for the go-carts. Who can ride them?

2. Only those 130 cm or taller can go on the roller coaster. Who is going for a ride?

3. Children 100 cm or taller can go on the ferris wheel. Who can go on that ride?

4. What is the range of the data?

BRAIN STRETCH

Lillian ran 1.4 km on Monday, 1.8 km on Wednesday and 2.1 km on Friday. How many km did she run altogether? How much farther did she run at the end of the week than at the beginning?

MONDAY Patterning and Algebra

1. Complete the pattern:

   4, 14, 24, _____, _____, _____

2. Complete the pattern:

   20, 40, 80 , _____, _____, _____

3. Each box holds 12 cookies. How many cookies in 6 boxes?

4. Find the missing number.

   200, 175, _____, 125, 100

5. Create a repeating pattern.

TUESDAY Number Sense

1. Put these fractions in order from greatest to least:

   $\frac{2}{8}$ $\frac{4}{8}$ $\frac{7}{8}$

2. Put these fractions in order from greatest to least:

   $\frac{2}{5}$ $\frac{1}{5}$ $\frac{3}{5}$

3. What fraction of this pie is shaded?

4. If Sue gave Jim half of an 8 piece chocolate bar, how many pieces would she have to give him?

5. Draw $3.20 using 5 coins.

WEDNESDAY Geometry and Spatial Sense

1. How many lines of symmetry?

   X

2. Name a polygon that has six vertices.

3. Name a polygon with 2 pairs of parallel lines.

4. Which pair of figures is congruent?

   A. 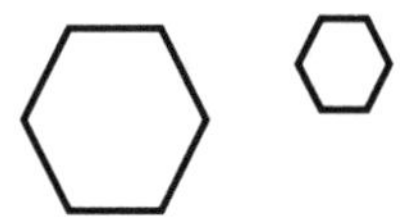 B. 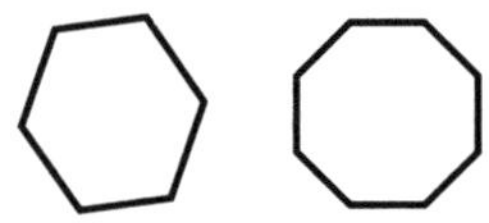

5. How many more vertices does a quadrilateral have than a triangle?

THURSDAY Measurement

1. What time is it?

2. The time is 2:15 pm.What time will it be in 55 minutes?

3. What is the perimeter of a rectangle 5 cm wide and 8 cm long?

4. What is the year 1 decade after 1934?

5. About how long would it take to brush your teeth?

   A. 4 mins B. 4 seconds C. 4 hours

FRIDAY Data Management

Everyone at Michael's school participated in a Winter Activity Day. Each person could choose the activity they wanted to do. This bar graph shows their choices.

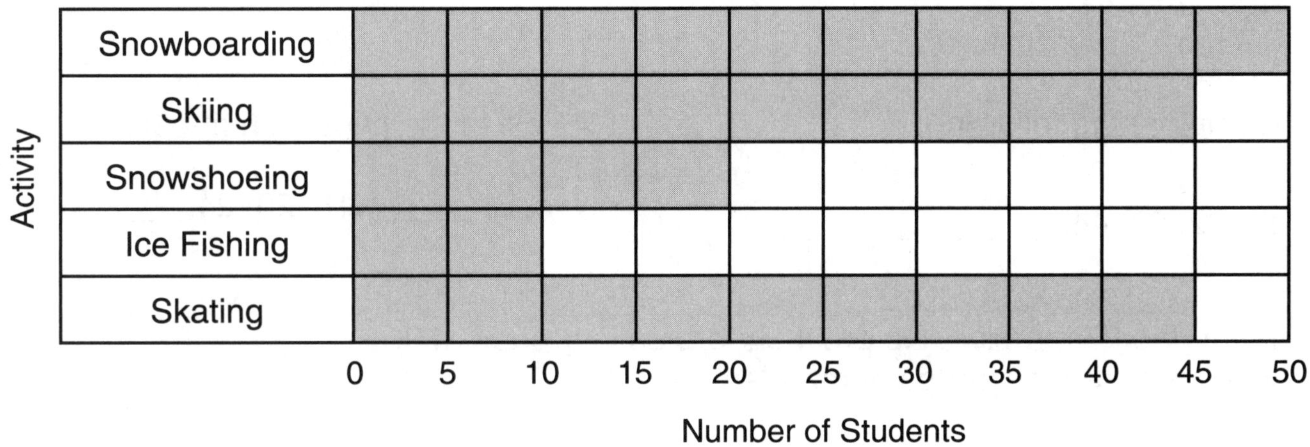

1. How many students participated in winter activity day? ____________

2. What was the most popular choice?____________

3. What was the least popular choice? ____________

4. What is the range of the data? ____________

5. How many people chose either skating or skiing? ____________

BRAIN STRETCH

Leonard delivers newspapers to 21 houses on Main St., 16 houses on Elm St. and 34 houses on Lincoln Ave. How many papers does he deliver altogether each day? How many papers does he deliver in a week?

MONDAY Patterning and Algebra

1. Create a repeating pattern:

2. 16 = 4 × _____

3. Complete the following:

   11, 22, 33, 44, _____, _____, _____

4. Fill in the missing numbers.

   4, 8, _____, 16, 20, 24,_____,

5. Luke had 27 marbles. He put the marbles in groups of 9. How many equal groups of marbles were there?

TUESDAY Number Sense

1. Put these fractions in order from least to greatest.

   $\frac{4}{5}$ $\frac{1}{5}$ $\frac{3}{5}$

2. Write four tenths in decimal form.

3. Write the following decimal as a fraction.

   0.57

4. What fraction of the pie is not shaded?

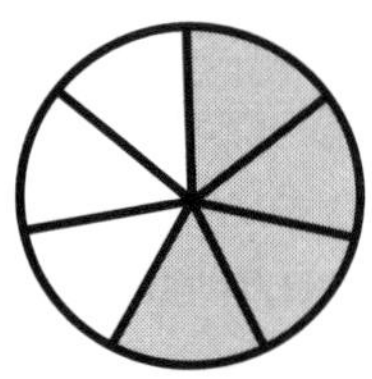

5. How much money?

   3 twenty-dollar bills, 3 toonies, 1 loonie, 3 quarters

WEDNESDAY Geometry and Spatial Sense

1. Classify the following angle.

2. How many sets of parallel lines does a triangle have?

3. How many vertices does a parallelogram have?

4. What is a polygon?

5. Which of the line segments on the trapezoid are parallel?

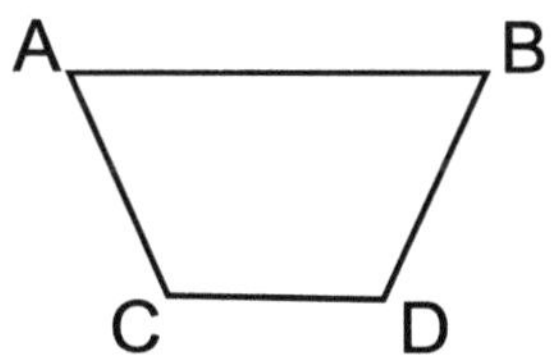

THURSDAY Measurement

1. What time is it?

2. The time is 4:05 pm. What time will it be in 55 minutes?

3.

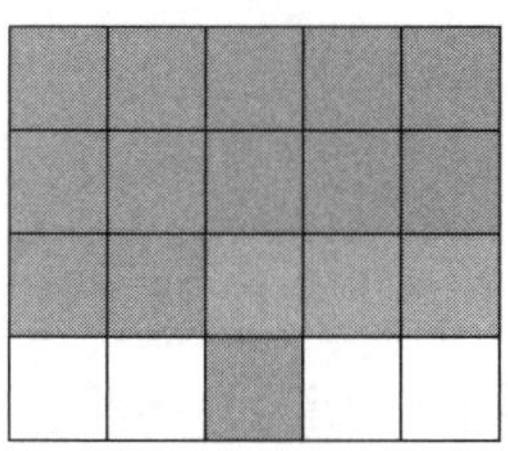

Perimeter = ________ units

Area = ______square units

4. Each week Ben plays soccer for 530 minutes. How many hours and minutes does he play soccer?

5. 6 km = ________cm

FRIDAY Data Management

Describe an event to match each probability:

1. impossible ______________________________

2. unlikely ______________________________

3. very likely ______________________________

4. certain ______________________________

BRAIN STRETCH

Melissa's family is traveling by train to Lewistown to see their aunt.

1. If each car is 11 m long, and there are 9 cars in their train, how long is the train they are traveling on?

2. Each car can hold 48 passengers. How many people can ride on the train at one time?

3. If they left their town at 9 am and are going to travel for 7 hours, when will they arrive at their destination?

MONDAY Patterning and Algebra

1. Create a shrinking pattern:

2. What are the next 5 terms in the pattern?

   1, 2, 2, 3, 3, 3, 4, 4, 4, 4,

3. Fill in the missing number in the pattern:

   19, 17, ___, 13, 11, 9

4. Is this a shrinking pattern?

   65, 60, 55, 50

5. Fill in the missing number in the pattern:

   11, 22, 33, ___, 55

TUESDAY Number Sense

1. Write ninety dollars in decimal form.

2. Write four hundred eighty dollars in decimal form.

3. Draw the money needed to represent $8.50.

4. If you had three ten dollar bills and five loonies, how much money would you have?

5. What is the value of the money?

WEDNESDAY Geometry and Spatial Sense

1. How many lines of symmetry?

L

2. What kind of lines do these line segments show?

3. Draw a pair of congruent shapes.

4. Classify the triangle as equilateral, isosceles or scalene.

5. Look at the shapes. Choose flip, slide, or turn.

THURSDAY Measurement

1. Find the area:

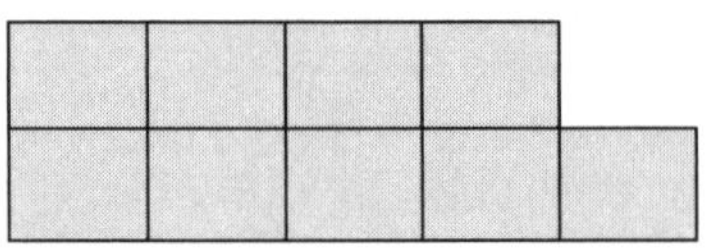

A = ____________________

2. What time is it?

3. Draw a pencil that is three centimetres long.

4. A book's mass is most likely:

   A. 500 g

   B. 500 kg

   C. 5 t

5. 1 kg = ______g

FRIDAY Data Management

The Eagles soccer team won every game this season. Here is a list of their scores:

1st game - 5	3rd game - 4	5th game - 2	7th game - 3
2nd game - 2	4th game - 2	6th game - 5	8th game - 2

1. What is the range of this data?

2. What is the most common score they got?

3. What is the highest score?

4. What is the lowest score?

BRAIN STRETCH

Charlie's friends want to see their favourite baseball team play this weekend. A ticket to the game costs $32.50.

1. How much will it cost for four people to attend the game?

2. If the game begins at 1:00pm and it takes the boys 1.5 hours to get to the field, when should they leave their houses?

3. If a program costs $5.25, how much change will someone get if they use a $10 bill to pay for it?

MONDAY Patterning and Algebra

1. Create a growing pattern:

2. 45 ÷ 9 = _____

3. 3 x _____ = 6

4. 

What will be the 25th figure in the pattern above?

5. 25 = _____ x _____

TUESDAY Number Sense

1. How much money is four loonies, six quarters, and two dimes?

2. How much money is eleven loonies, five dimes, and six nickels?

3. Draw a combination of bills and coins for $23.65.

4. Draw a combination of bills and coins for $89.15.

5. If Spencer spent half of his $44.00 savings, how much did he spend?

WEDNESDAY Geometry and Spatial Sense

1. How many right angles does a rectangle have?

2. How many faces does a rectangular prism have?

3. Are these shapes congruent or similar?

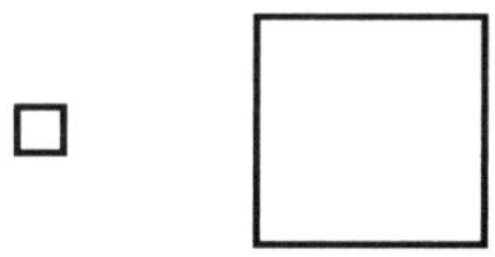

4. What shape is the face of a cylinder?

5. Draw a 90 degree angle.

THURSDAY Measurement

1. What is the perimeter of the rectangle?

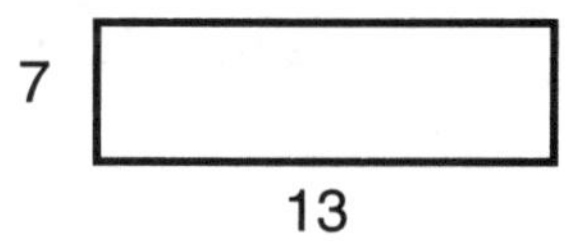

2. What time is it?

3. 24.5 m =______cm

4. Draw a square with an area of 25 cm^2.

5. How many years in 4 decades?

FRIDAY Data Management

Mary has 10 marbles in her pocket: 3 black, 2 red, and 5 yellow.

1. What is the probability of picking a yellow marble?

2. What is the probability of picking a black marble?

3. What is the probability of choosing a red marble?

4. What is the probability of picking a marble?

5. What is the probability of choosing a blue marble?

BRAIN STRETCH

One orange costs $0.60, or you can buy a dozen for $5.95.

1. Which is the better price? Explain.

2. If you bought one dozen oranges and used a five dollar bill and a toonie to pay for your purchase, what would your change be?

MONDAY Patterning and Algebra

1. Create a pattern:

   starts at 3, multiply by 2

2. 50 = ____ x 5

3. Extend the pattern.

   5, 6, 7, 5, 6, 7,_____, _____, _____

4. Are the sums equal?

   7 + 6   5 + 8

5. Create a shrinking pattern.

TUESDAY Number Sense

1. What is the place value of 7 in the number 8763?

2. What number comes after 2341?

3. What number comes before 908?

4. Madelyn is the eighth in line. How many people are in front of her?

5. Multiply:

$$\begin{array}{r} 68 \\ \underline{\times\ 7} \end{array}$$

WEDNESDAY Geometry and Spatial Sense

1. What is a straight angle?

2. How many lines of symmetry?

   H

3. How many faces does a pyramid have?

4. Draw a pair of intersecting lines.

5. Can you make a cube with this net?

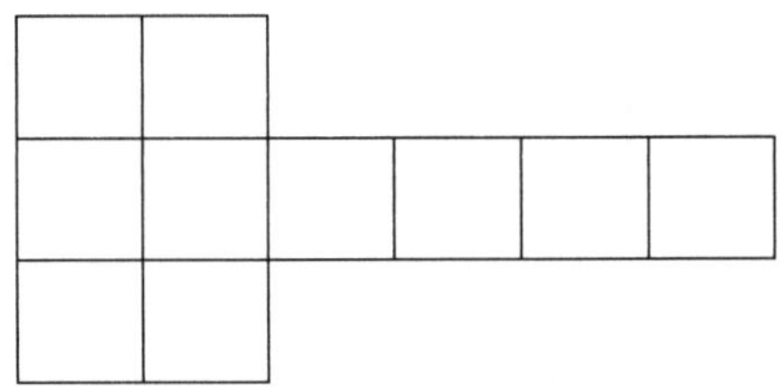

THURSDAY Measurement

1. 400 dm = ______ km

2. What measuring tool would you use to measure the height of your room?

3. A cup of tea is about:
   A. 1 L
   B. 1ml
   C. 250ml

4. 72 hours = _____days

5. How long might it take you to write your name?

FRIDAY Data Management

Here are the results of a Favourite Breakfast Food Survey.
Complete the chart and answer the questions about the results.

Favourite Breakfast Foods	Tally	Number
Cereal		17
Eggs		15
Pancakes		25
Grilled Cheese Sandwich		12

1. What was the most popular breakfast food? ________________

2. What was the least popular breakfast food?________________

3. How many people liked either cereal or pancakes? ________________

4. How many people liked pancakes more than eggs? ________________

BRAIN STRETCH

Steve has a mass of 41 kg. Nick's mass is 44.5 kg and Tyler's mass is 38.2 kg.

1. How much heavier is Nick than Steve?

2. How much lighter is Tyler than Steve?

3. What is their total mass?

MONDAY Patterning and Algebra

1. 45 x ____ = 90

2. 60 – 5 = ____

3. 

What kind of pattern is this?

4. What will be the 20th figure?

5. Extend the pattern:

1 1 2 2 3 3 4 4 1 1 2 2 3 ____, ____, ____, ____

TUESDAY Number Sense

1. Write a fraction equivalent to ½.

2. Write a fraction equivalent to ¾.

3. Which fraction is larger?

¼ ⅔

4. Which fraction is larger?

¾ ½

5. Which fraction is larger?

⅗ ½

WEDNESDAY Geometry and Spatial Sense

1. A trapezoid has one pair of parallel sides.

   true or false

2. Draw a straight angle.

3. How many right angles does a trapezoid have?

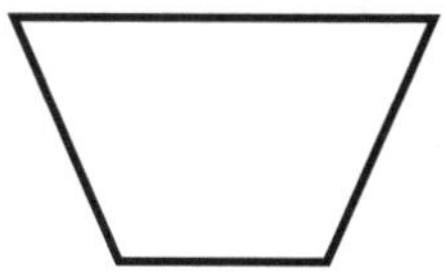

4. Are these shapes congruent or similar?

5. How many faces does a cylinder have?

THURSDAY Measurement

1. Draw a rectangle that has a side 2 cm long.

2. Sunita can walk to school in 18 minutes. If she leaves at 8:10 am, when will she arrive at school?

3. Find the area of a square that has 3 cm sides.

4. 20 dm = ___ cm

5. How many years in a century? In a millennium?

FRIDAY Data Management

Use the calendar to answer the questions.

June

Sunday	Monday	Tuesday	Wednesday	Thursday	Friday	Saturday
				1	2	3
4	5	6	7	8	9	10
11	12	13	14	15	16	17
18	19	20	21	22	23	24
25	26	27	28	29	30	

1. How many Saturdays are in the month of June? ______________
2. What day of the week is June 9th? ________________
3. Name the date that is 2 weeks after June 13th. ______________
4. What is the date on the third Sunday in June? ______________
5. What day of the week does the month end on? ______________

BRAIN STRETCH

The Lemington Lions basketball team had a great season. They scored 26 points during their first game, 22 points during their second game, 33 points during their third game, 40 points during their fourth game and 34 points during their last game.

1. How many points did they score all season?

2. What is the range of their points scored?

MONDAY Patterning and Algebra

1. 25 x ___ = 225

2. Extend the pattern:

   2, 5, 8, 11, ____, ____, ____

3. Are the sums equal?

   11 + 14   19 + 8

4. Find the first four numbers of the pattern:

   start at 7, add 4

5. Extend the pattern:

   4, 7, 10, 13, ____, ____, ____

TUESDAY Number Sense

1. Name 3 composite numbers.

2. Name 3 prime numbers.

3. Multiply:

$$\begin{array}{r} 512 \\ \underline{\times\ 3} \end{array}$$

4. Multiply: 19 x 8

5. Megan has two sets of hockey cards. Each set has nine cards. How many cards does she have altogether?

WEDNESDAY Geometry and Spatial Sense

1. Draw an obtuse angle.

2. Draw an acute angle.

3. How many lines of symmetry does the following letter have?

U

4. 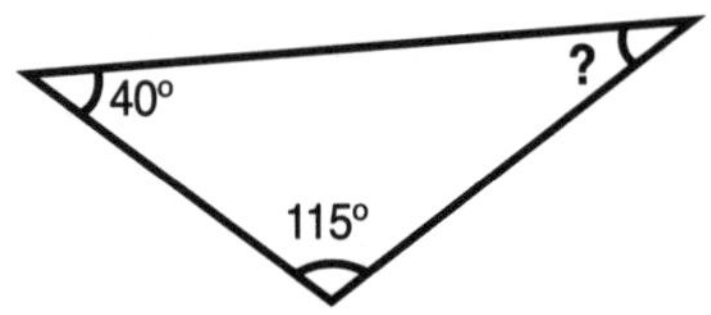

measure of angle ______________

type of triangle ________________

5. Reflect this shape

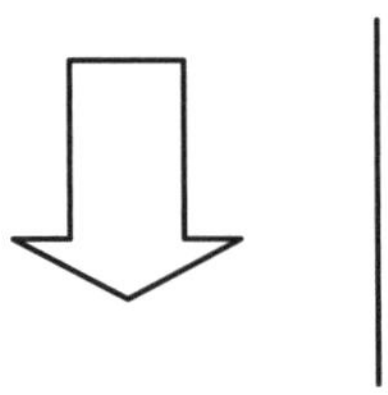

THURSDAY Measurement

1. 42 days = _______ weeks

2. Michael went to do his homework at 8:15 pm and finished at 9:18 pm. How long did it take?

3. Compare the following using: >, < or =

18 cm ☐ 180 mm

4. How long does it take to tie your shoes:

1 hour 1 min 1 day

5. Find the perimeter of this shape.

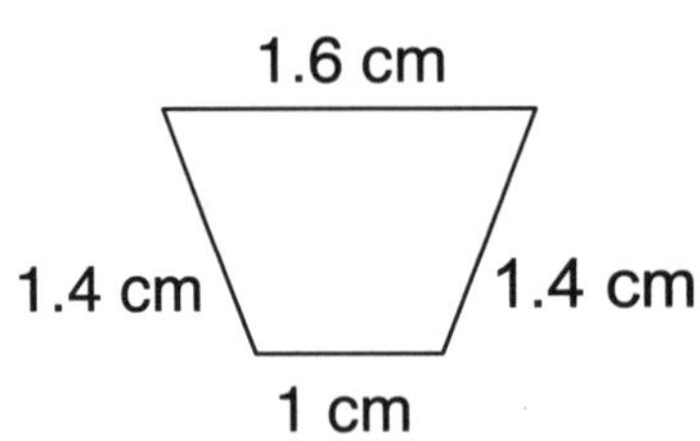

FRIDAY Data Management

Ben went fishing. Look at the chart to see the number of fish Ben caught over a Monday to a Friday.

Day of the Week	Monday	Tuesday	Wednesday	Thursday	Friday
The Number of Fish Caught	5	10	15	20	25

1. On what day did Ben catch the most number of fish? ________________

2. On what day did Ben catch the least number of fish? ________________

3. How many fish did Ben catch on Tuesday and Thursday? ______________

4. What is the difference between the most number of fish Ben caught and the least number of fish? ________________

BRAIN STRETCH

Can you name three 3D shapes that can roll? Draw them.

MONDAY Patterning and Algebra

1. Create a shrinking pattern.

2. Make the statement true:

   30 + _____ = _____+10

3. Are these differences equal?

   30 - 18   20 - 6

4. Extend the pattern:

   144, 134, 124, 114, ______, ______, ______

5. What is the pattern rule for question number 4?

TUESDAY Number Sense

1. Divide:

   42 ÷ 7 =

2. Divide:

   62.9 ÷ 10 =

3. Multiply:

   5 x 9 =

4. Divide:

   $6\overline{)420}$

5. A basket holds eight pears. How many pears do six baskets hold?

WEDNESDAY Geometry and Spatial Sense

1. How many faces does a cube have?

2. Are these shapes similar or congruent?

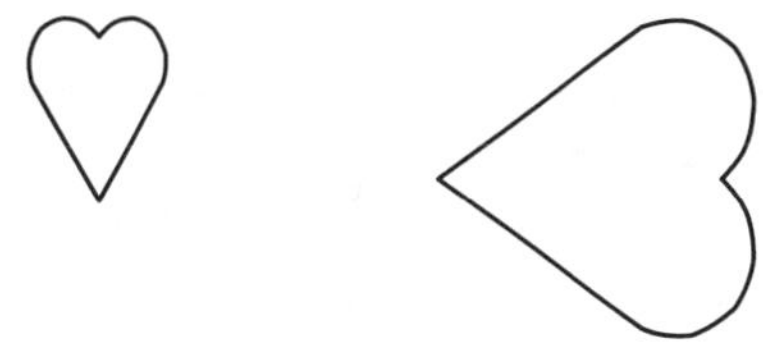

3. How many inside obtuse angles does a pentagon have?

4. What 3D figure can be made with these pieces?

5. Draw a pair of congruent shapes.

THURSDAY Measurement

1. What measuring tool would you use to find the mass of your body?

2. Find the area of this rectangle:

6 cm

3.6 cm

3. A bucket can hold about:
   A. 6 L of water
   B. 6 drops of water
   C. 6 ml of water

4. Katelyn took 3 hours and 20 minutes to finish reading a book. How many minutes was that in total?

5. 2 years = ________ weeks

FRIDAY Data Management

Here are the results of a Favourite Sport Survey.
Complete the chart and answer the questions about the results.

Sport	Tally	Number
Basketball		18
Baseball		9
Football		7
Soccer		15

1. What was the most popular sport? ________________

2. What was the least popular sport? ________________

3. How many people liked either soccer or football?____________

BRAIN STRETCH

Madelyn practices the violin for 6.5 hours a week.

1. How many hours a month does she practice?

2. How many hours a year does she practice?

MONDAY Patterning and Algebra

1. Fill in the missing number:

   6,9,12,_____,18,21,24

2. 60 = 25 +_____

3. Complete the pattern:

   1,2,4,8,16, _____,

4. Find the first five numbers of the pattern rule:

   start at 17, add 3

5. Write a number sentence that equals 81 ÷ 9 = 9.

TUESDAY Number Sense

1. Multiply:

   23.6 X100

2. Divide:

   56 ÷ 8 =

3. Divide:

   261.8 ÷ 100 =

4. A horse has four legs. How many legs do eleven horses have?

5. Subtract:

$$\begin{array}{r} \$94.87 \\ \underline{-\ \$32.38} \end{array}$$

WEDNESDAY Geometry and Spatial Sense

1. Classify the angle.

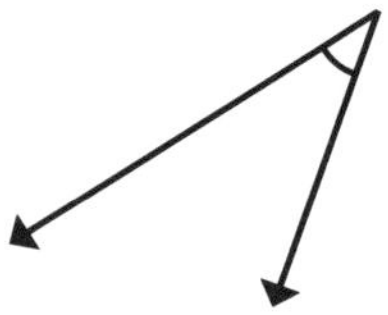

2. Classify the angle.

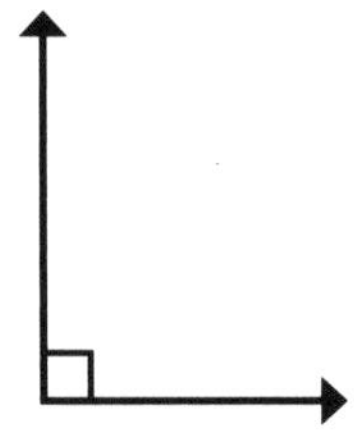

3. Draw the reflection:

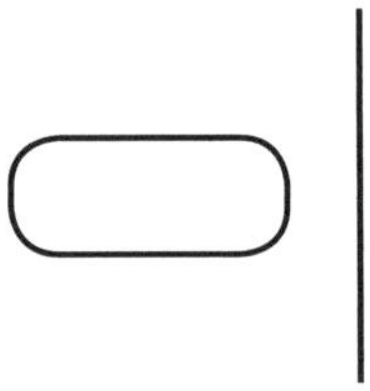

4. Draw a net for a pyramid.

5. How many edges does a rectangular prism have?

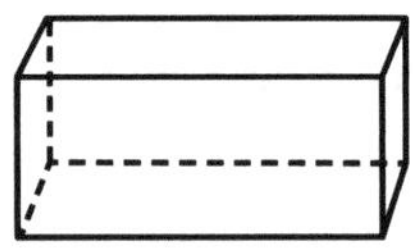

THURSDAY Measurement

1. Find the area of this shape.

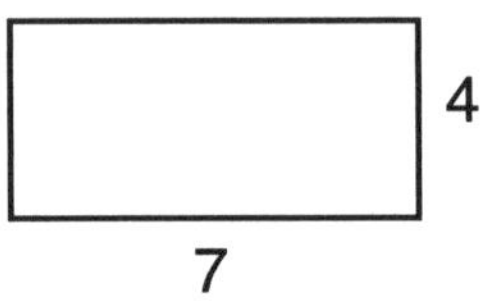

2. A bicycle is likely:

   A. 20 kg

   B. 20 g

   C. 20 mg

3. 60 years = ___ decades

4. Liam walked 1.4 km to the beach. How many metres did he walk?

5. Draw a line that is 45mm long.

FRIDAY Data Management

Mr. Wellars computer class recorded their typing speeds. Here is a list of how many words per minute they can type:

12	**16**	**11**	**12**	**14**	**20**
11	**19**	**17**	**11**	**17**	**12**
16	**18**	**12**	**19**	**19**	**12**

1. What is the range of the data?

2. What is the mode?

3. What is the fastest speed in the class?

4. What is the slowest speed in the class?

5. How many students are in the class?

BRAIN STRETCH

Jennifer, Laura and Karen were buying supplies for a school project. They bought a sheet of Bristol board for $1.75, a glue stick for $2.30, markers for $3.55 and construction paper for $1.95.

1. How much did they spend altogether?

2. How much will each girl have to spend?

MONDAY Patterning and Algebra

1. Are the quotients equal?

   36 ÷ 4   28 ÷ 7

2. Complete the pattern:

   225, 230, 235, 240, ______, ______, ______

3. Complete the pattern:

   109, 105, 101, 97, ______, ______, ______

4. 80 - 61=

5. What is the pattern rule?

   1000, 900, 800, 700, 600

TUESDAY Number Sense

1. A bicycle has two wheels.
   How many wheels do six bikes have?

2. Madelyn is 9th in line to get a drink after lunch. How many people are in front of her?

2. Multiply:

   4 x 6=

3. Gum is sold in packs of eight pieces. How many pieces are in three packs?

4. Name three odd numbers between 50 and 100.

WEDNESDAY Geometry and Spatial Sense

1. Name two quadrilaterals.

2. How many faces does a rectangular prism have?

3. Classify the angle.

4. How many acute angles does a trapezoid have?

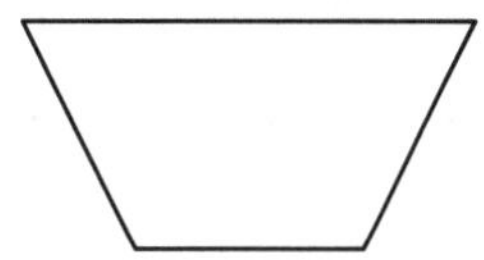

5. 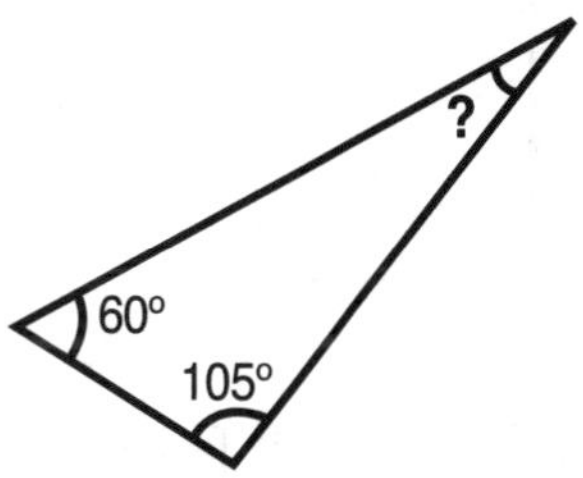

measure of angle ___________

type of triangle______________

THURSDAY Measurement

1. Complete the following using >,< or =:

   56 km ☐ 5000 m

2. Find the perimeter of the octagon.

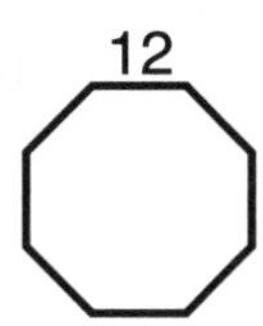

3. John delivers newspapers after dinner for 3.5 hours. If he starts at 6:15 pm, when will he finish?

4. What time is it?

5. 80 minutes =______hours ______minutes

FRIDAY Data Management

Lawrence surveyed kids in his grade to find out what type of books they liked to read. Here are his results:

Fiction 25 Non-Fiction 12 Science-Fiction 5 Comic Books 22 Joke Books 26

Create a tally chart to show the results.

Fiction	Non-fiction	Science Fiction	Comic Books	Joke Books

1. What is the most popular type of book?
2. What is the least popular type of book?
3. What are the top three types of books?
4. How many people did Lawrence ask?
5. What is the range of the results?

BRAIN STRETCH

Two times a number, plus 15, is 31. What is the number?

MONDAY Patterning and Algebra

1. What is the missing number?

   _____ ÷ 21 = 7

2. 180 - _____ = 65

3. What will be the 16th shape in the pattern?

4. Complete the pattern:

   3, 10, 17, 24, ___, ___, ___

5. What kind of pattern is this?

   122333444455555

TUESDAY Number Sense

1. Divide:

   36 ÷ 9 =

2. Round to the nearest thousand

   8725

3. Write the equivalent fraction.

   $\frac{3}{10} = \frac{\quad}{20}$

4. Choose >, <, or =.

   2122 ☐ 1221

5. Madelyn bought 5 bunches of tulips. Each bunch cost $3.20. She paid with $20.00. What was Madelyn's change?

WEDNESDAY Geometry and Spatial Sense

1. Can a cube be made from this net?

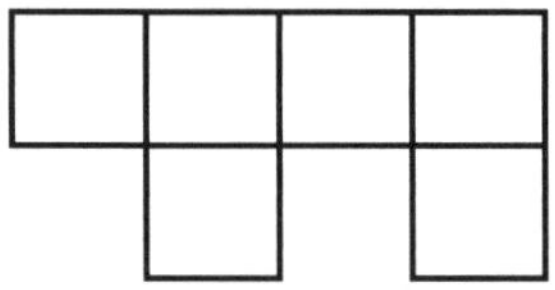

2. Draw a pair of similar shapes.

3. How many triangular faces does a triangular prism have?

4. How many lines of symmetry?

P

5. Which pair of lines are not parallel?

A. 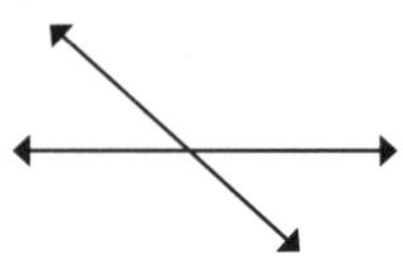

B. 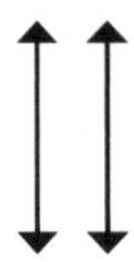

C. 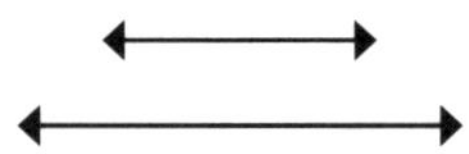

THURSDAY Measurement

1. 220 mm = ____cm

2. What measuring device would you use to find a cup of milk?

3. Megan's dog weighs 10 kg. How many grams is that?

4. 2100 ml = ____L

5. Compare the following using: > ,< or =

120 mins ☐ 1.5 hours

FRIDAY Data Management

Stacy worked at The Olde Ice Cream Shoppe in the summer. She kept a tally of all the sales she made and created this pictograph from her results.

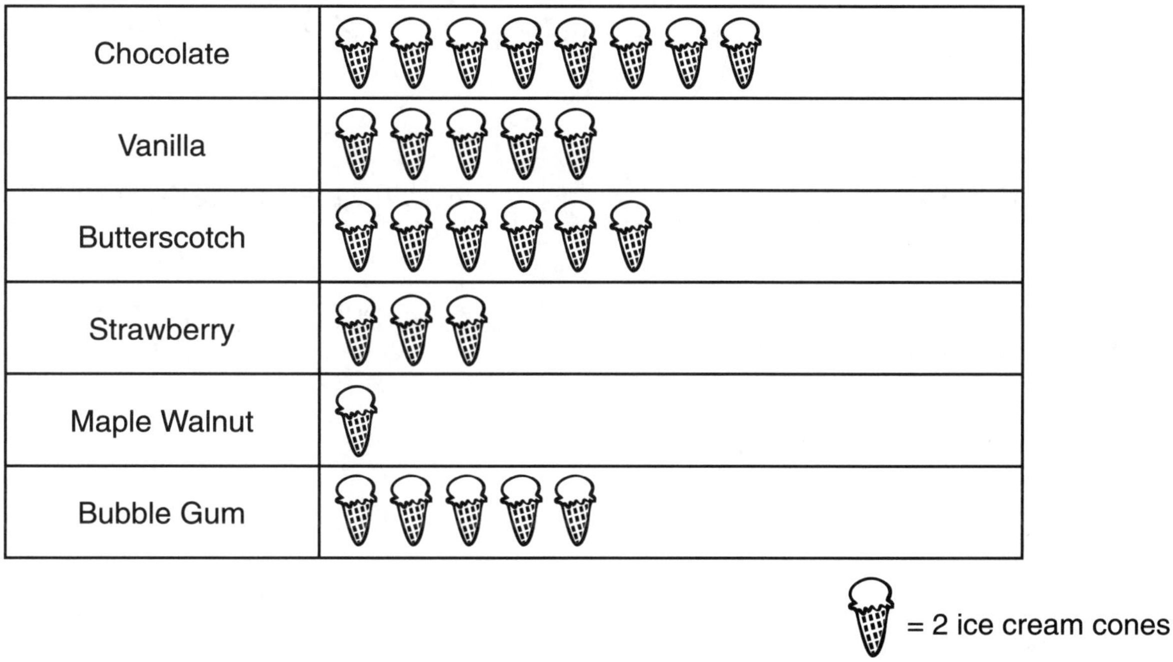

1. What was the most popular flavour?

2. What was the least popular flavour?

3. Which two flavours sold the same amount?

4. How many purchases were made on the day the survey was taken?

5. What is the range of the data?

BRAIN STRETCH

How much money in total?

3 twenty-dollar bills, 1 toonie, 3 loonies, 3 quarters, 4 dimes, and 9 nickels

MONDAY Patterning and Algebra

1. Write the following in another way.

   8 + 8 + 8 + 8

2. Are the products equal?

   7 x 6   4 x 12

3. _____ x 6 = 54

4. What is the pattern rule?

   900, 850, 800, 750

5. What kind of pattern is this?

   105, 115, 125, 135, 145, 155

TUESDAY Number Sense

1. Divide:

   $4\overline{)29}$

2. Divide:

   $3\overline{)35}$

3. How many quarters are in 10 loonies?

4. Subtract:

   145 – 91 =

5. Shelly had 27 shells. She put the shells in groups of 5.
   How many equal groups of shells were there?

WEDNESDAY Geometry and Spatial Sense

1. Name a polygon with 5 vertices.

2. Which shape has 2 pairs of parallel lines and all sides are equal?

3. Draw a 180 degree angle.

4. Can a cone be made from this net?

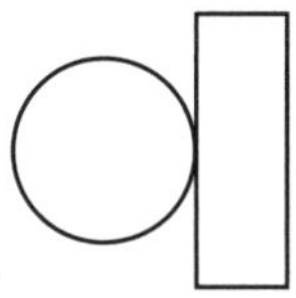

5. 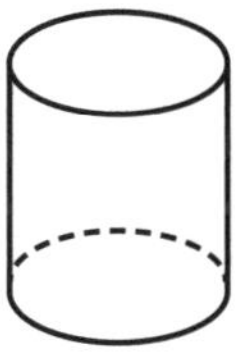 This is a ______________________.

How many? faces _______ edges______ vertices ______

THURSDAY Measurement

1. Would you measure the contents of a bathtub using ml or L?

2. What temperature is it most likely to be if you are outside playing in the snow?

   A. – 5°C

   B. 30°C

   C. 4°C

3. Spencer brushes his teeth twice a day for 2 minutes. How many minutes does he brush his teeth each week?

4. How many decades in 5 centuries?

5. It is 4:00 pm. What time will it be in 1 hour and 14 minutes?

FRIDAY Data Management

Emily's mom brought a bag of fruit to the family picnic. She put: 3 bananas, 5 apples, 10 apricots, and 2 mangoes in the bag. What is the probability of randomly selecting the following?

What is the probability as a fraction of:

1. a banana
2. a mango
3. an apple
4. an apricot or mango
5. a chocolate bar

BRAIN STRETCH

How many of these nets can be made into cubes?

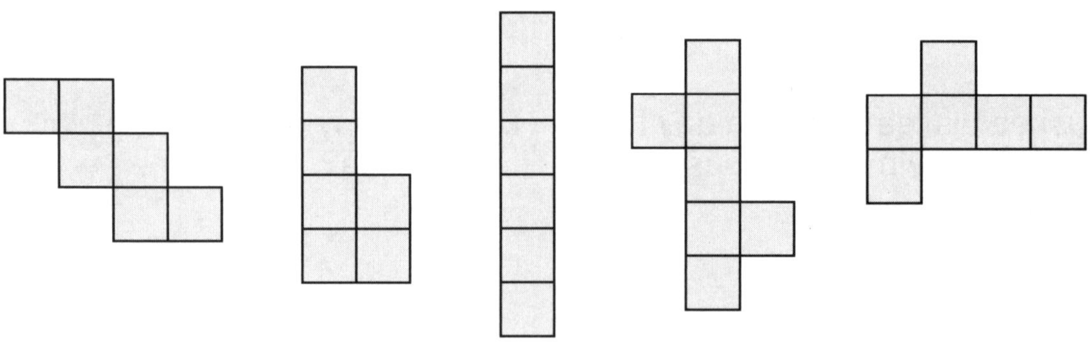

MONDAY Patterning and Algebra

1. 45 ÷ 5 = 21-____

2. Extend the pattern:

   55, 61, 67, 73, ___, ___, ___

3. Quadrilaterals are shapes with 4 sides.

   true or false

4. Find the first four numbers of the pattern rule:

   start at 202, add 6

5. What will be the 12th number in this pattern?

   4, 8,12,16, 20, 24

TUESDAY Number Sense

1. Divide:

   106 ÷ 2=

2. What is 124 divided by 4?

3. There were 30 children. 19 of the children were boys. What fraction of the children were girls?

4. What is 81 divided by 3?

5. Vicki wants to share her twenty jelly beans equally with her best friend. How many can each have?

WEDNESDAY Geometry and Spatial Sense

1. Is a 120 degree angle obtuse, acute or right?

2. How many faces does a cylinder have?

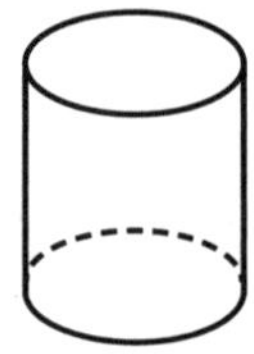

3. Draw a reflection of this shape:

4. How many triangular faces does a cube have?

5. Classify the following pair of lines.

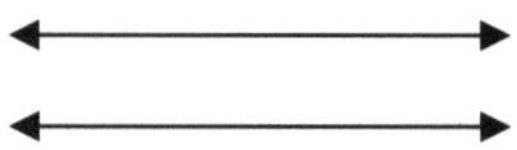

A. intersecting   B. parallel   C. perpendicular

THURSDAY Measurement

1. 3305 m=______ km

2. Draw a rectangle with an area of 18 units^2.

3. 6 months = _____ weeks

4. The best estimate of the weight of Ben's frog is:

   A. 50 g
   B. 5 g
   C. 1500 g

5. Spencer can hop on one foot for 200 seconds. How many minutes is that?

FRIDAY Data Management

Here is a pie graph to show students' favourite seasons.

Students' Favourite Season

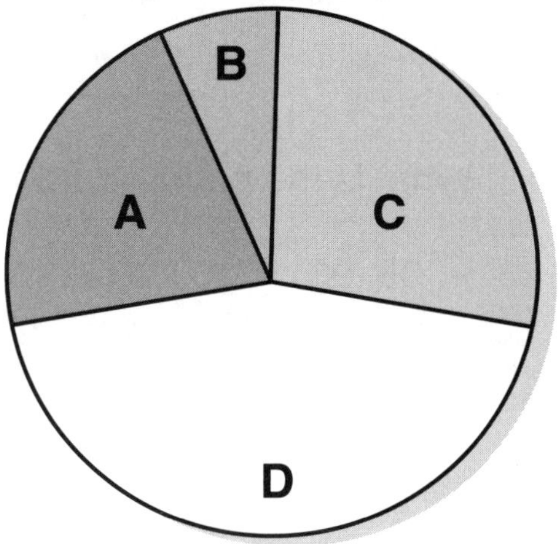

A - Spring
B - Fall
C - Winter
D - Summer

1. Which season was picked the most?

2. Which season was picked the least?

3. Which two seasons were picked about the same?

BRAIN STRETCH

A dozen eggs cost $1.20. How much do 10 dozen eggs cost?

MONDAY Patterning and Algebra

1. Extend the pattern:

   100, 99, 97, 94, _____, _____, _____

2. What is the next shape in the pattern?

3. Are the products equal?

   3 x 8 4 x 6

4. What is the pattern rule?

   99, 93, 87, 81, 75

5. 55 x _____ = 110

TUESDAY Number Sense

1. Susan bought three skirts for $9.95 each. How much was the total bill?

2. Add:

$$\begin{array}{r} 2778 \\ +4619 \\ \hline \end{array}$$

3. Subtract:

$$\begin{array}{r} 81\,730 \\ -\ 14\,458 \\ \hline \end{array}$$

4. Chris gave 630 hockey cards to his friends. He gave the same number of cards to each of his 10 friends. How many cards did each friend get?

5. What is the difference between 8.4 and 2.6?

WEDNESDAY Geometry and Spatial Sense

1. Show a line of symmetry on this shape:

2. Can a cube be made from this net?

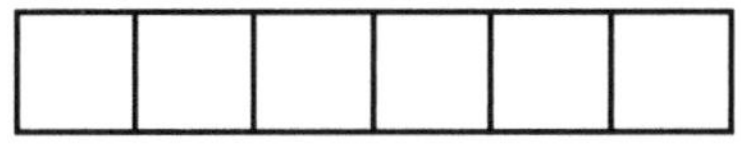

3. Are these shapes similar or congruent?

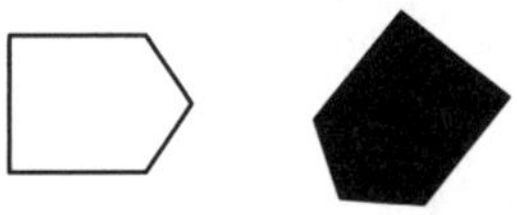

4. How many right angles can a triangle have?

5. Look at the shapes. Choose flip, slide, or turn.

THURSDAY Measurement

1. Kristine's family is going on a vacation for 3 weeks. How many days is that?

2. Find the perimeter of a pentagon whose sides are 2.2 m long.

3. What measuring tool would you use to find the width of a car?

4.

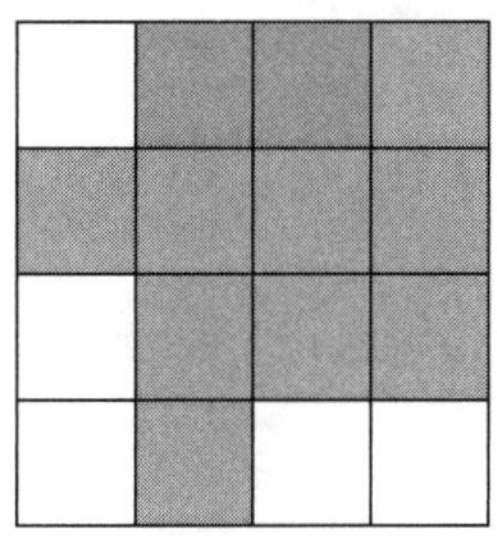

Perimeter = ________ units

Area = _______square units

5. 30 km =________ m

FRIDAY Data Management

Mrs. Carter's class regularly exercises to stay fit. They counted how many push ups they can do in a minute. Here are their results:

11	5	16	28	20	11
8	8	15	11	9	15
20	24	21	11	19	12

1. What is the range of the data collected?

2. What is the mode?

3. How many students were surveyed?

4. What is the greatest number of push ups done in one minute?

5. What is the least number of push ups done in a minute?

BRAIN STRETCH

Michael bought 4 boxes of holiday cards. Each box has 18 cards.

1. How many cards were there altogether?

2. If he paid $24.96, how much was each box?

MONDAY Patterning and Algebra

1. Are these differences equal?

   65 - 12   77 - 21

2. Make this statement true:

   33 + ___ = 50 - 10

3. Complete the pattern:

   5, 13, 21, 29, ____, ____, ____

4. What is the missing number?

   ☐ x 100 = 900

5. Show the first five numbers of this pattern:

   start at 60, subtract 7

TUESDAY Number Sense

1. Arrange these digits to make the smallest possible number.

   6 9 2 4

2. Write $43.89 in words.

3. What is the following decimal as a fraction?

   0.67

4. What is the sum of 4.2 and 5.9?

5. Sam has eighty-one trading cards. He has twelve more than John. How many cards does John have?

WEDNESDAY Geometry and Spatial Sense

1. Draw two lines of symmetry on this shape.

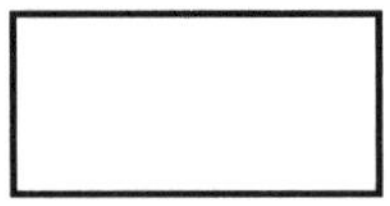

2. How many sides of equal length does a square have?

3. Draw a set of parallel lines.

4. How many vertices does this shape have?

5. A soda can is what kind of 3D figure?

   A. cube

   B. cone

   C. cylinder

THURSDAY Measurement

1. 2 years = ______ days

2. Find the area of this shape:

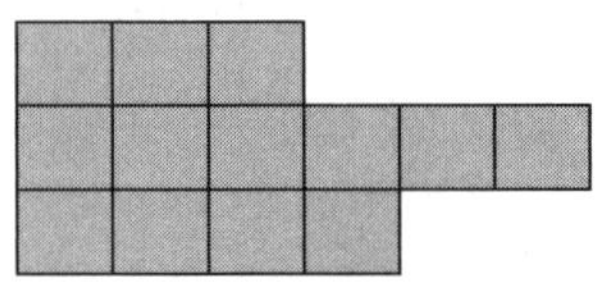

3. Draw a worm that is 25 mm long.

4. Compare the following using: >,< , or =

   11 minutes ☐ 200 seconds

5. Draw a square with a perimeter of 24 units.

FRIDAY Data Management

Students at Orchard Park Public School can choose any event to participate in during the school's annual Spring Field Day. Here are some of the choices:

Standing Long Jump	45 students
High Jump	14 students
Shot Put	31 students
Running Long Jump	38 students
100 m Sprint	60 students
1500 m Run	38 students

1. How many students were surveyed?

2. What was the most popular event?

3. What was the least popular event?

4. How many students chose either shot put or 100 m sprint?

5. What is the range of the data?

BRAIN STRETCH

Sophie's favourite CD has 10 songs on it. Its total length is 39 minutes. On average, how many minutes was each song?

MONDAY Patterning and Algebra

1. What is the pattern rule?

   60, 75, 90, 105, 120

2. Are the products equal?

   6 x 8 11 x 4

3. In which number sentence does a 10 make the equation true?

   A. 8 x ___ = 48

   B. 18 ÷ ___ = 2

   C. 190 + ___ = 200

4. Create a growing pattern.

5. 100 = 25 + 20 + ____

TUESDAY Number Sense

1. Divide:

   64 ÷ 8 =

2. Draw the least amount of coins needed to represent $7.70.

3. What is $\frac{89}{100}$ as a decimal?

4. Multiply:

   3.9 x 100 =

5. Mary got $12.25 back in change when she bought markers. She paid with a twenty dollar bill. How much did the markers cost?

WEDNESDAY Geometry and Spatial Sense

1. How many edges does a cylinder have?

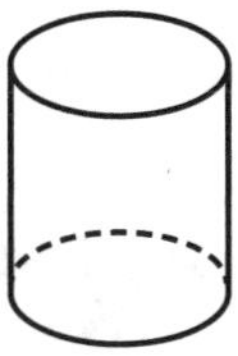

2. Draw an acute angle.

3. Draw a straight angle.

4. Draw two lines of symmetry on this shape:

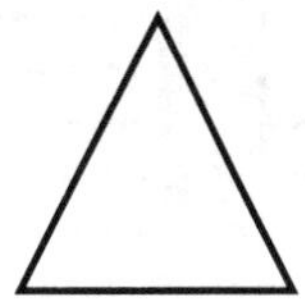

5. How are a circle and triangle different?

THURSDAY Measurement

1. Compare the following using: >,<, or =

   2 kg ☐ 1098 g

2. Lisa carries a lot of books home from school. Her backpack most likely weighs about:

   A. 10 kg

   B. 10 g

   C. 0 mg

3. Robin's birthday is six days after Valentine's Day. When is her birthday?

4. 6 dm =_____mm

5. 2680 g = _______ kg

FRIDAY Data Management

Here is a bar graph of how much money the grade 4 class fund raised for a class trip.

Trip Fund Raising

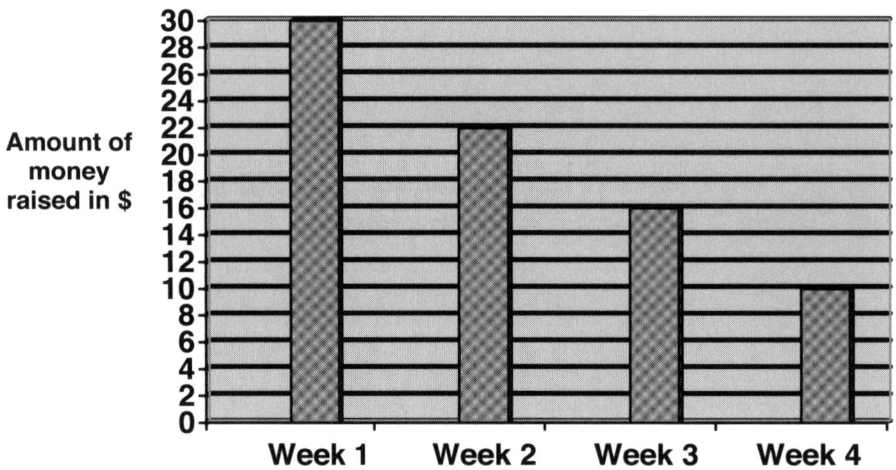

1. What week was the most money raised? _______________

2. How much money was raised in week 2? ________________

3. How much money was raised altogether? _______________

4. How much more money was raised in week 3 than in week 4? ____________

BRAIN STRETCH

Farmer Felipe has a large corn field measuring 30 m by 24 m. He wants to build a fence around it.

1. How many square metres of corn can he plant?

2. What is the perimeter of the field?

3. If fencing costs $8 per metre, how much will his fence cost altogether?

MONDAY Patterning and Algebra

1. What are the first six numbers of this pattern?

   start at 220, subtract 11

2. Fill in the blank to make the statement true.

   5 X 12 = 70 - ___

3. In which number sentence does a 7 make the equation true?

   A. 3 x ___ = 18

   B. 28 ÷ ___ = 4

   C. 24 + ___ = 35

4. What is the pattern rule?

   2,13, 24, 35, 46, 57

5. Complete the pattern:

   89, 88, 87, 89, _____, _____, _____

TUESDAY Number Sense

1. Order these numbers from greatest to least:

   8901, 9801, 8109

   ______, ______, ______

2. Choose >, <, or =.

   98 ☐ 89

3. Round 2398 to the nearest thousand.

4. What fraction is shaded?

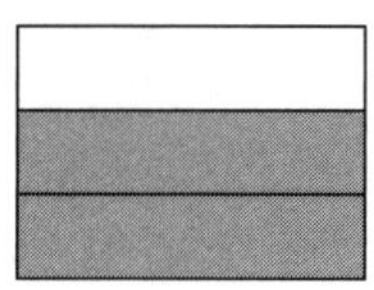

5. Add:

   $\frac{4}{8} + \frac{3}{8} =$

WEDNESDAY Geometry and Spatial Sense

1. How many lines of symmetry?

   E

2. Is a 91 degree angle obtuse, acute or right?

3. How many faces does a sphere have?

4. Draw a line of symmetry on this shape:

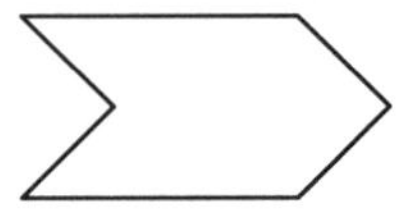

5. Draw the faces of a triangular based pyramid.

THURSDAY Measurement

1. What is the area of a square that has 7 dm sides?

2. Beatrice bathes four times a week. How many times does she bathe in a year?

3. 360 seconds = ________ minutes

4. What measuring tool would you use to find the depth of a kitchen sink?

5. Draw a square with a perimeter of 20 units.

FRIDAY Data Management

Henry surveyed his neighbours to see which newspapers they subscribed to. Here are his results:

Telegram	18
Mirror	25
Daily	9
None	4

1. Create a pictograph below using the data in the space above. What symbol will you use to represent a paper? What key will you use?

BRAIN STRETCH

Divide a number by 8, subtract 2, and multiply it by 4. The result is 32. What is the number?

MONDAY Patterning and Algebra

1. Fill in the blank to make the statement true.

   2 x 12 =_____ x 6

2. Complete the pattern:

   67, 65, 63, 61, _____, _____, _____

3. Are the quotients equal?

   54 ÷ 9   49 ÷ 7

4. What will be the 8th number in this pattern?

   7, 14, 21, 28, 35

5. In which number sentence does a 9 make the equation true?

   A. 3 x ___ = 24
   B. 18 ÷ ___ = 2
   C. 24 + ___ = 30

TUESDAY Number Sense

1. Subtract;

   $\frac{4}{6} - \frac{1}{6} =$

2. Add:

   398 + 125 =

3. Write 2745 in words.

4. How many legs do six spiders have?

5. Divide:

   $4\overline{)28}$

WEDNESDAY Geometry and Spatial Sense

1. How many right angles does a square have?

2. Reflect this shape.

3. How many vertices does a sphere have?

4. How many angles are in a circle?

5. Draw an obtuse angle.

THURSDAY Measurement

1. What would be the best estimate of how many litres of water could fit in a pitcher?

    A. 1 L
    B. 10 L
    C. 100 L

2. Which has a greater mass: a horse or a dog?

3. What is the perimeter of a hexagon with 5 m sides?

4. 410 cm =______ dm

5. How many days in 6 years?

FRIDAY Data Management

Mr. Lewis posted the class marks for the science test. Here are the results:

88	**90**	**76**	**30**	**90**
100	**100**	**88**	**90**	**20**
80	**72**	**100**	**88**	**100**
48	**100**	**86**	**76**	**98**

1. What is the highest mark?

2. What is the lowest mark?

3. What is the mode?

4. How many students wrote the test?

5. What is the range of the marks?

BRAIN STRETCH

Gerry ordered eight pizzas for his birthday party. Each pizza had ten slices.

1. How many pieces of pizza will there be altogether?

2. If there are 18 people at his party, how many pieces of pizza can each person have?

MONDAY Patterning and Algebra

1. Create a repeating pattern.

2. Show the first 3 numbers in this pattern:

   start at 200, subtract 15

3. In which number sentence does 4 make the equation true?

   A. 20 x ___ = 80

   B. 18 ÷ ___ = 2

   C. 24 + ___ = 30

4. What will be 14th number in this pattern?

   54, 51, 48, 45, 42, 39

5. Fill in the blank to make the equation true.

   40 – 9 =______+ 23

TUESDAY Number Sense

1. Divide:

   128.9 ÷ 1000=

2. Write six tenths in numbers.

3. Order these numbers from least to greatest.

   345, 545, 435, 334

   ______, ______, ______, ______

4. 8 novels cost $40. How much does each novel cost?

5. Name the factors for 72.

WEDNESDAY Geometry and Spatial Sense

1. A scalene triangle has 3 equal sides.

   true or false

2. Draw a figure that does not have a line of symmetry.

3. Draw a trapezoid.

4. Are these shapes similar?

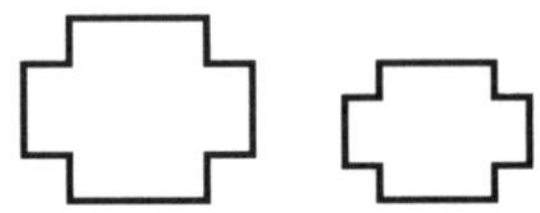

5. Draw a pair of congruent shapes.

THURSDAY Measurement

1. Find the perimeter of a hexagon with 4 mm equal sides.

2. 96 hours = _____ days

3. Draw a rectangle with an area of 72 square units.

4. Draw a letter N that is 3 cm tall.

5. Connor has a 30 minute piano lesson each week. How many hours of lessons does he have in six months?

FRIDAY Data Management

Here is a graph of the most popular types of movies this holiday:

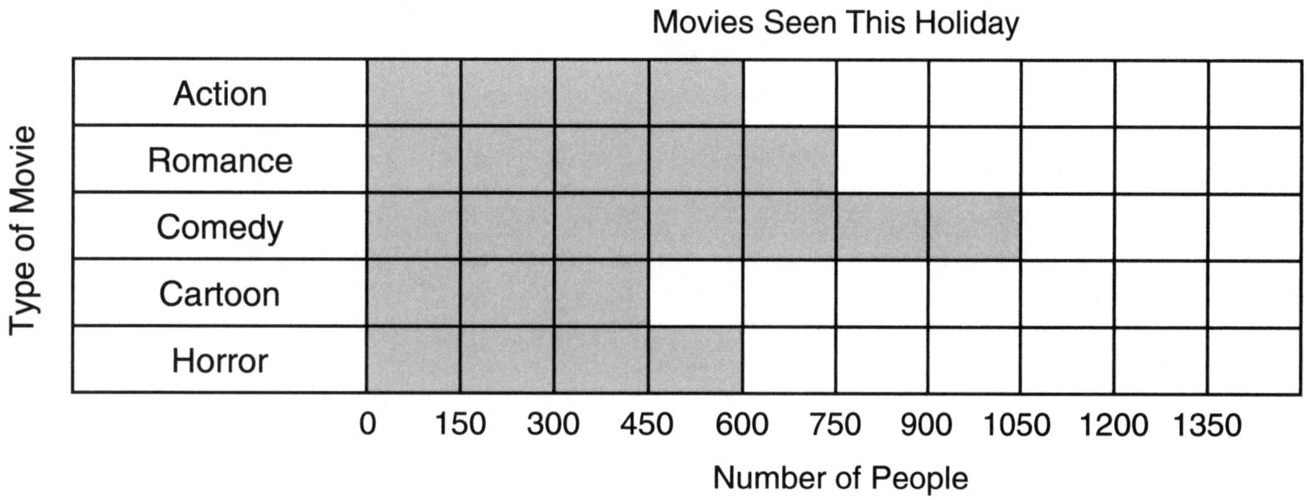

1. What is the range of the data?

2. What is the most popular type of movie?

3. What is the median?

4. What two types of movies did people like the same?

5. How many people went to the theatre altogether during the holiday?

BRAIN STRETCH

David and Demetra went for a 4 km bike ride. How many metres did they ride?

MONDAY Patterning and Algebra

1. What is the missing number?

   ______ ÷ 12 = 144

2. Are the products equal?

   3 x 9   4 x 8

3. 66 - _____ = 30 + 20

4. What is the pattern rule?

   32, 36, 40, 44, 48, 52

5. John runs 3 km every day. How many km will John run in 45 days?

TUESDAY Number Sense

1. Name the factors for 48.

2. Divide:

   $6\overline{)38}$

3. Write 67 523 in expanded form.

4. What number is 10 less than 48 352?

5. Multiply:

   99 x 100 =

WEDNESDAY Geometry and Spatial Sense

1. Can you make a pyramid with this net?

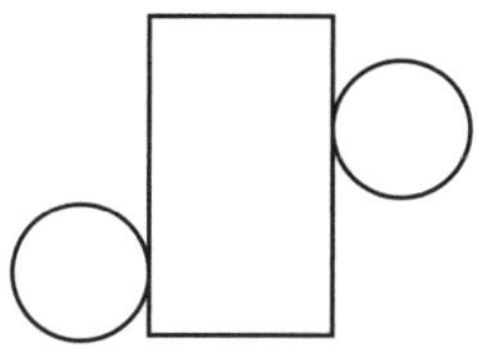

2. An equilateral triangle has 3 equal sides.

   true or false

3. How many edges does a rectangular prism have?

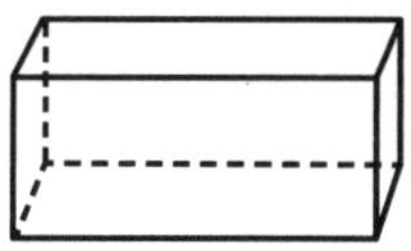

4. Draw the reflection of this shape:

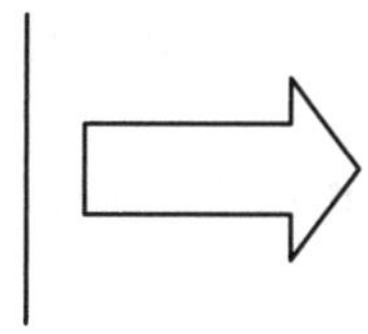

5. What does congruent mean?

THURSDAY Measurement

1. 11 cm =_______m

2. Compare the following using: >, < or =

   3.5 ☐ 5.3

3. Rob plays video games for 20 minutes each day. How long does he play in four weeks?

4. What is the area of this rectangle?

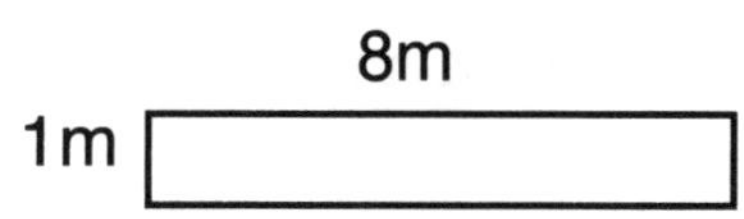

5. What measuring device would you use to find the length of a movie?

FRIDAY Data Management

Answer the probability questions using the information on the two spinners.

Spinner 1

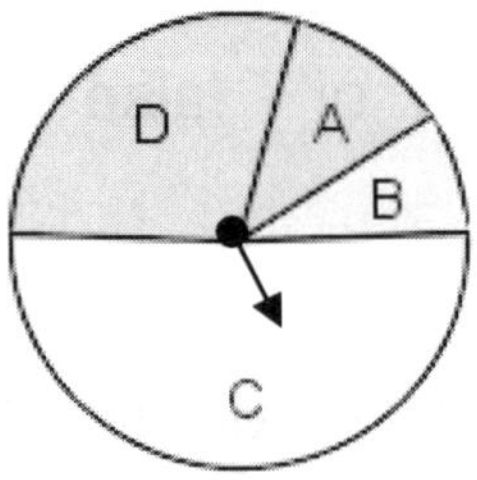

Spinner 2

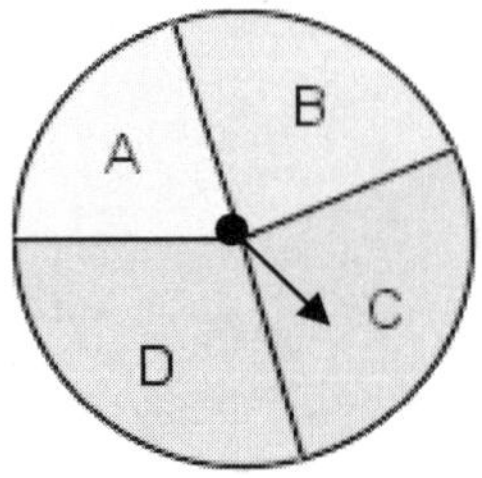

If someone has only 1 spin:

1. Is spinning C more probable on Spinner 1 or Spinner 2? ________

2. On which spinner is A more probable? __________

3. On which sipnner is B less probable? ___________

4. Which letter is equally likely on both Spinner 1 and Spinner 2? _________

BRAIN STRETCH

Elizabeth's hockey team won 12 games and lost 3 games this season.

1. How many games did they play altogether?

2. If Elizabeth's mother had to pay $3 to watch her games, how much did she have to pay for the season?

3. Her hockey team will play three times as many games next year. How many games will that be?

Math—Show What You Know!

- [ ] I read the question and I know what I need to find.
- [ ] I drew a picture or a diagram to help solve the question.
- [ ] I showed all the steps in solving the question.
- [ ] I used math language to explain my thinking.

FANTASTIC EFFORT!

You are a MATH MASTER!

____

Name

Math Glossary

A

* **Words** = problem solving words

Above: In or at a place that is higher.

Acute: An angle that measures less than 90°.

Acute Triangle: A triangle with three acute angles.

Addend: Any number used to add to get a sum. In 7 + 2 = 9, the addends are 7 and 2.

Addition: An operation where two or more numbers are combined.

Algebra: An area of math where numbers are represented by letters.

Algebraic Expression: A mathematical phrase that can have numbers, letters, and operation signs. It does not have an equal sign.

Algorithm: A set of steps to follow for carrying out a calculation.

Always: At all times.

Amount: A quantity, number of, total, sum, or size

Analogue Clock: A tool used to show the time. It has moving hands and hours marked from 1 to 12.

Angle: The figure formed when two lines meet at a vertex.

Approximately: to come close to or be nearly the same as.

Area: The space a surface takes up. Area is measured in square units.

Array: Numbers or objects arranged in rows and columns.

Attribute: A characteristic that describes something. Colour and size are examples.

Axis: Real or imaginary reference line. *X*-axis: the horizontal axis of a graph. *Y*-axis: the vertical axis of a graph.

B

Bar Graph: A graph that uses horizontal or vertical bars to show data.

Base Ten: A number system based on ten.

Behind: At the back or rear.

Below: In or at a place that is lower than another object.

Benchmark: A standard by which something can be measured. A reference to help judge.

Beside: At the side of or next to.

Between: In a space that separates objects or times.

Broken Line Graph: A graph that uses points to show data. The points are sometimes connected with a line.

C

Calculate: To figure out by computation.

Cardinal Direction: The main points of a compass—north, east, south, and west.

Cartesian Plane: A plane containing two perpendicular axes (x and y).

Capacity: The amount a container can hold.

Celsius: A temperature measurement scale used in the metric system. For example 0° is the temperature of freezing water.

Centimetre: A metric unit used for measuring length. 100 cm = 1 m

Math Glossary

* **Words** = problem solving words

Century: A period of time equal to 100 years.
Certain: An event that will definitely happen.
Chance: The likelihood that a particular outcome will happen.
Circle Graph: A graph that uses a circle divided into sectors to represent data. Also called a pie chart.
Circumference: The distance around a circle. Circumference = 2 × 3.14 × radius, or $C = 2\pi r$.
Classify: To arrange and order.
Clock: A tool that measures and shows time.
Collect: To bring together.
Compare: To find what is the same and what is different about numbers or objects.
Conclusion: The result or outcome of an act or process.
Constant: A number that does not change.
Coordinates: The values in an ordered pair that can be shown on a coordinate grid.
Coordinate Systems: An ordered pair of numbers that show location.
Concrete Graph: A graph where real objects are used to represent data.
Congruent: Having the same shape and size.
Coin: A piece of metal used as money.

D

Data: A collection of information that is often shown on tables or graphs.
Decade: A period of time equal to 10 years.
Decimal Point: The point which separates the integer and fraction parts of a number.
Decimal System: A number system that is based on 10. Also called the base 10 system.
Decomposition: A way to separate a number into parts.
Decrease: To get smaller.
* **Define:** State the meaning of something.
Degree: A unit for measuring the size of angles. For example 60°
Denominator: The number of parts that a whole is divided into. It is the bottom number of a fraction.
* **Describe:** Express an idea using words, numbers, and pictures.
* **Determine:** To find out exactly.
Diagram: A drawing that represents something.
Diameter: A straight line passing through the centre of a circle touching two points on the edge of the circumference.
Difference: The result of subtraction.
Digit: A symbol used to make a number. 0, 1, 2, 3, 4, 5, 6, 7, 8, and 9 are the digits we use to make numbers such as 12.
Dime: A Canadian or an American coin valued at 10 cents.
Discrete Data: Data that has a certain number of possible values.
Distance: The length between points.
Division: An operation where a quantity is grouped into equal parts. See multiplication for definition.
Double: Twice as much.

Math Glossary

E

* **Words** = problem solving words

Edge: Where two faces of a 3D object meet.
Elapsed Time: The measured duration of an event.
Equal: Having the same value.
Equality: The state of being equal.
Equation: A mathematical sentence that uses an equal sign that shows two expressions are equal.
Equilateral: Having all sides or faces equal.
Equivalent Fractions: Fractions that have the same value but may have different numerators and denominators.
Estimate: To approximate an answer. Rounding is an example.
Even Number: A number that can be divided evenly by two.
Event: Possible outcome(s) in an experiment.
Expanded Form: A way of writing numbers that shows the value of each digit. An example is 200 + 40 + 1.
Experiment: A test to discover something unknown, or to verify something expected.
* **Explain:** To offer reasons and/or to justify.
Expression: One or a group of mathematical symbols representing a number or quantity.

F

Face: One surface of a 3D object.
Factors: Numbers that are multiplied to produce a product.
Fair: When events are equally likely.
Favourable Outcome: Positive results.
Few: A small number.
Flip: To turn over.
Fraction: A number that represents part of a group or a whole.
Frequency: The number of times an event occurs.

G

Graph: A drawing or diagram used to record information.
Greater Than: More than.
Grouping: Dividing things into equal groups or sets.
Growing Pattern: A pattern where the terms become larger.

H

Height: A measurement from top to bottom.
Horizontal: Parallel to the horizon.
Hour: A unit of time that is equal to 60 minutes.

Math Glossary

* **Words** = problem solving words

I

* **Investigate:** To explore or research by problem solving.
Impossible: An event that cannot happen.
Improper Fraction: A fraction whose numerator is larger than the denominator.
Increase: To get larger.
Inequality: Not equal in size, amount or value.
Interpret: To translate or analyze.
Intersecting Lines: Two lines that cross.
Interval: The distance between two points.
Inverse Operations: Two operations that are opposite. Addition is the opposite of subtraction. $2 + 3 = 5$ $5 - 2 = 3$
Isosceles: A triangle with two equal sides and two angles the same size.

J

* **Justify:** To support or defend.

K

Kilogram: A metric unit for measuring mass (weight). 1 kilogram (kg) = 1000 grams (g)
Kilometre: A metric unit for measuring distance (km). 1 kilometre (km) = 1000 metres (m)

L

Least: The smallest number in a group or a set of data.
Length: The measurement of distance between two points.
Less: Not as many as another number.
Likelihood: A chance that an outcome will happen.
Likely: An event that is expected to happen more than half the time.
Line: A length (straight or curved) without breadth or thickness.
* **List:** To itemize or tally.
Litre: A metric unit of capacity.
Location: The place or position of an object.

M

Many: Opposite of few.
Mass: The quantity of matter in an object often measured in grams or kilograms.
Mean: The sum of a set of values divided by the number of values in the set.
It is also referred to as average.

Math Glossary

* **Words** = problem solving words

Measure: Using standard units to find a size or a quantity.

Median: The middle value in an ordered set of values. The values are lined up in order from the smallest to the largest to find the middle value.

Metre: A metric unit used for measuring length.

Metric System: A decimal system of measurement using multiples of ten.

Millennium: A period of time equal to 1000 years.

Millimetre: A metric unit for measuring length. 10 mm = 1 cm

Mixed Number: A number written as a whole number and a fraction.

Mode: The most frequently occurring value in a set of values.

More likely: An event that will probably occur.

More: The greater amount.

Most: The greatest amount.

Multiplication: An operation where a number is added to itself a number of times.

N

Net: A flat shape that can be folded into a 3D object.

Never: Absolutely not. The probability is zero.

Nickel: A Canadian or an American coin valued at 5 cents.

Non standard: Objects such as paper clips used as measurement units.

Numerator: The number above the line in a fraction.

O

Obtuse Angle: Any angle between 90° and 180°.

Obtuse Triangle: A triangle with one obtuse angle.

Odd Number: A number that cannot be divided evenly by two.

Operation: In math there are four operations to solve problems: addition, subtraction, multiplication, and division.

Ordered Pair: A pair of numbers used to locate a point on a coordinate grid. An example is (9, 12).

Ordinal Number: A number that shows a place or position.

Outcome: The different ways that an event can happen in a probability experiment.

P

Parallel: Lines that are the same distance apart and never meet.

Parallelogram: A quadrilateral where the opposite sides are parallel and equal in length.

Pattern: An arrangements of shapes, numbers, or objects that repeat.

Penny: An American coin valued at 1 cent.

Pentagon: A polygon with five sides.

Perimeter: The distance around a shape or an object.

Pictograph: A graph that shows data using pictures.

Math Glossary

* **Words** = problem solving words

Place Value: The value of a digit depending on its position in a number.

Polyhedron: Three dimensional figures with plane faces.

Polygon: A closed shape having three or more sides.

* **Predict:** Describe what may happen based on the information provided in the question.

Primary Data: Data observed or collected directly from first-hand knowledge.

Prime Number: A whole number that has only two factors. It can be divided evenly only by one and itself. (2, 3, 5, 7, and 11 are some examples)

Prism: A 3D object with two bases that are parallel and congruent.

Probability: The chance or likelihood of something happening.

Probably: An event that might occur.

Product: The answer when two numbers are multiplied. The product of 2 and 4 is 8.

Pyramid: A 3D object with a polygon as a base and triangular faces that taper to the same vertex.

Q

Quadrant: Any quarter of a plane divided by an *x* and *y* axis.

Quadrilateral: A polygon having four sides.

Quantity: Amount of something.

Quarter: A Canadian or an American coin valued at 25 cents.

Quotient: The answer after dividing one number by another one. For example, the quotient of 6 ÷ 2 is 3.

R

Range: The difference of the highest number and lowest number in a set of data.

Ray: A line that has a starting point but no endpoint.

Ratio: A comparative value of two or more amount. An example is 2:4 or as a fraction.

Reasoning: Evidence or arguments used in thinking or forming conclusions.

Reciprocal: One of two numbers whose products are 1.

Rectangle: A quadrilateral with four right angles and two pairs of opposite equal parallel sides. Length and width can be either equal or unequal.

Rectangular Prism: A prism with rectangular faces.

Reflection: A mirror image of a shape or an object.

Remainder: The amount left over after dividing a number.

Represent: To show.

Rhombus: A type of quadrilateral, a parallelogram with four equal sides and opposite angles.

Right Angle: An angle which is equal to 90°.

Right Angled Triangle: A triangle with one angle measuring 90°.

Rotation: A circular movement where a central point is fixed and everything else moves around that point.

Rotational Symmetry: The shape or image is rotated and still looks the same. This image can be rotated to three different positions and it would always look the same.

Round: To change a number to a more convenient number. For example, to round 22 to the nearest 10 is 20.

Math Glossary

S

* **Words** = problem solving words

Scalene: A triangle where no sides are equal.

Secondary Data: Data collected by someone other than the user.

Set: A collection of items.

Sequence: An ordered set of numbers, shapes, or other mathematical objects that are arranged according to a rule.

* **Show Your Work:** Use pictures, words, numbers, diagrams, symbols, and graphs to show your thinking as you arrived at your solution.

Side: One of the lines that make up a 2D shape.

Simplify: To reduce the numerator and denominator in a fraction or to the smallest numbers possible.

Skeleton: An outline or sketch.

Skip Count: Counting forward or backward using a specific multiple or interval.

Slide: To move an item in direction without rotating it.

Sort: To organize according to shape, colour, or number.

Square-Based Pyramid: A pyramid with a square base.

Square: A quadrilateral with four equal sides, four right angles, four lines of symmetry, and the opposite sides are parallel.

Standard: Using a measurement unit as a means for measure.

Stem and Leaf Plot: A data display where groups of data are arranged by place value.

* **Strategy:** A plan, or way to solve a problem or get to an answer.

Subtraction: An operation where one number is taken away from another number.

Sum: The result of addition.

Surface area: Total area of a surface of a 3D figure and is measured in square units.

Survey: A method of collecting data.

Symmetry: An object has symmetry if one half of the object is a mirror image of the other half.

T

Table: An organizer that shows data in rows and columns.

Tally: Using marks to record counts or votes.

Tangram: An ancient Chinese puzzle based on a square cut into seven pieces.

Temperature: A measurement of how hot or cold something is.

Tenth: One part of ten equal parts.

Term: One of the numbers in a sequence or series of numbers.

Three-Dimensional Object: A figure that has height, depth, and width. Written as 3D.

Time: Time is the ongoing sequence of events taking place. Time is measured using clocks and other timing devices.

Transformation: A change in position or size.

Translation: Also called a slide, moves every point on a shape in the same direction and distance.

Triangular Prism: A polyhedron, a prism with two identical triangular bases.

Turn: To rotate.

Two-Dimensional Shapes: A shape that has only width and height and no thickness. Written as 2D.

Math Glossary

* **Words** = problem solving words

U

Unit: Another name for one.

Unlikely: An event that is expected to happen less than half the time.

V

Value: A numerical amount.

Variable: A quantity that can change. It is a symbol for a number that has not been determined yet. An example is *x*.

Venn diagram: A diagram using circles or other shapes showing relationships among sets of data.

Vertex: An example is *x* in 2D geometry, where two lines meet. In 3D geometry, where three or more edges meet. The plural of vertex is vertices.

Vertical: In an up-down position.

Volume: The amount of space an object occupies. Volume is measured in cubic units.

W

Weight: The measure of how heavy something is.

Whole Number: Any number used for counting including zero.

Width: The distance across from one side to the other.

X

***x*-axis:** The horizontal axis of a graph.

***x*-coordinate:** The position of a point along the *x*-axis. The *x*-coordinate is written first in an ordered pair of coordinates (*x*,*y*).

Y

***y*-axis:** The vertical axis of a graph.

***y*-coordinate:** The position of a point along the *y*-axis. The *y*-coordinate is written second in an ordered pair of coordinates (*x*,*y*).

Answers

Counting by 5s and 25s Page 4

1. 10, 15, 20, 25, 30 **2.** 160, 165, 170, 175, 180, 185 **3.** 735, 740, 745, 750, 755, 760 **4.** 270, 265, 260, 255, 250, 245 **5.** 855, 850, 845, 840, 835, 830 **6.** 995, 990, 985, 980, 975, 970 **7.** 300, 325, 350, 375, 400 **8.** 225, 250, 275, 300, 325, 350 **9.** 575, 550, 525, 500, 475

Counting by 10s Page 5

1. 30, 40, 50, 60, 70, 80 **2.** 143, 153, 163, 173, 183, 193 **3.** 234, 244, 254, 264, 274, 284 **4.** 496, 506, 516, 526, 536, 546 **5.** 3462, 3472, 3482, 3492, 3502, 3512 **6.** 90, 80, 70, 60, 50, 40 **7.** 881, 871, 861, 851, 841, 831 **8.** 3230, 3220, 3210, 3200, 3190, 3180

Brain Stretch a) 200 b) 300 c) 500 d) 700

Counting by 100s and 1000s Page 6

1. 300, 400, 500, 600, 700 **2.** 320, 420, 520, 620, 720, 820 **3.** 415, 515, 615, 715, 815, 915 **4.** 227, 327, 427, 527, 627 727 **5.** 402, 502, 602, 702, 802, 902 **6.** 2000, 3000, 4000, 5000, 6000, 7000 **7.** 3150, 4150, 5150, 6150, 7150, 8150 **8.** 4249, 5249, 6249, 7249, 8249, 9249 **9.** 3009, 4009, 5009, 6009, 7009, 8009 **10.** 4652, 5652, 6652, 7652, 8652, 9652

Growing Number Patterns Page 7

1. a) 9, 18, 27, 36, 45, 54, 63 b) 14, 21, 28, 35, 42, 49, 56 **2.** 6 **3.** Add 8 each time.

Shrinking Number Patterns Page 8

1. a) 27, 24, 21, 18, 15, 12, 9 b) 40, 35, 30, 25, 20, 15, 10 **2.** a) 4 b) 8

3. a) Subtract 7 each time. b) Subtract 6 each time.

Extending Patterns Page 9

1. a) +4, +3, +4; 49, 53, 56; Start at 32. Add 3, then add 4. b) +5, +2, +5, +2; 93, 95, 100; Start at 74. Add 5, then add 2. c) -2, -3, -2, -3 ; 28, 25, 23; Start at 40. Subtract 2, then subtract 3. d) -10, -5, -10, -5; 25, 20, 10; Start at 65. Subtract 10, then subtract 5. **2.** Answers will vary. Example: 5, 7, 6, 8, 7; Start at 5. Add 2, then subtract 1; 9, 8, 10

3. 1, 3, 9, 27 **4.** 76, 72, 68, 64, 60. After six days, Omar has 60 bars left.

Brain Stretch Julie's pattern is correct. Brian didn't include the "add 5" part of the rule. Mason didn't indicate which number the pattern should start at, or include "add 5".

Using a Table of Values Page 11

1. a) 8, Start at 2 and add 2 each time. b) 16, Start at 1 and add 5 each time. c) 18, Start at 3 and add 5 each time d) 21, Start at 3 and add 6 each time. **2.** a) Start at 3. Add 3.; 15 b) Start at 2. Add 3 each time.; 14

Comparing and Ordering Numbers Page 13

1. Just before: 200; Just after: 1400; Just before and after: 3200, 3400; Between: 689; Just after: 430 **2.** a) 469 should be circled b) 594 should be circled c) 2294 should be circled d) 3411 should be circled e) 537 should be circled f) 1456 should be circled g) 959 should be circled h) 2122 should be circled **3.** a) 345, 435 b) 538, 549 c) 2348, 2349 d) 2399, 3421 e) 5421, 5423 f) 6110, 6210 g) 899, 989 h) 342, 432 **4.** a) 123, 95, 84 b) 289, 245, 212 c) 3254, 2546, 2134 d) 5278, 5189, 4259 e) 543, 435, 324, 234 f) 1879, 1532, 1456, 1346 **5.** a) 1000 less than b) 1000 more than c) 1000 less than d) 1000 less than **6.** a) 4298 > 4199 b) 9239 < 9299 c) 10567 < 10657 d) 12298 > 11289 e) 23458 < 24267 f) 43320 > 42230 **7.** a) 853 b) 954 **8.** a) 2347 b) 1358

Thousands, Hundred, Tens, and Ones Page 16

1. 2, 2, 1, 8, 2218 **2.** 3, 6, 3, 7, 3637 **3.** 1, 5, 3, 3, 1533 **4.** 2, 2, 3, 1, 2231 **5.** 0, 4, 1, 5, 415 **6.** 1, 5, 0, 4, 1504 Brain Stretch [image of 1 thousand block, 2 hundred blocks, 3 ten blocks and 4 one blocks] **7.** 1, 6, 4, 3, 1643 **8.** 3, 3, 5, 0, 3350 **9.** 2, 1, 6, 7, 2167 **10.** 1, 5, 3, 9, 1539

Explore Place Value Page 19

1. b) 20 c) 0 d) 600 e) 400 f) 4000 **2.** a) 2, 3, 4, 7 b) 4, 5, 9, 6 c) 9, 8, 7, 5 **3.** a) 3000 + 400 + 70 + 6 b) 6000 + 200 + 50 + 8 **4.** 1 stands for 10000, 3 stands for 300, 4 stands for 40, 5 stands for 5.

What's the Value? Page 20

1. a) 9 b) 3 c) 7000 d) 7 e) 3000, 40 **2.** a) 400 b) 4000 c) 4 d) 40
Brain Stretch a) 1804 > 1728 b) 2430 < 3375 c) 6664 < 6668 d) 7891 = 7891

Writing Numbers Different Ways Page 21

1. 1140 + 1 and the words should be circled. **2.** The blocks and words should be circled. **3.** The words and blocks should be circled. **4.** The words and numbers should be circled. **5.** The words and the numbers should be circled. **6.** The words and numbers should be circled.

Writing Numbers in Standard Form Page 22

1. 248 **2.** 3000 **3.** 4392 **4.** 7263 **5.** 1302 **6.** 8213 **7.** 9856 **8.** 2189 **9.** 4650 **10.** 45 **11.** 6439 **12.** 2581

Writing Number Words Page 23

1. b) one thousand two hundred thirty-four c) two thousand four hundred sixty-five d) one thousand three hundred ninety e) twelve thousand one hundred twenty-five f) fifty thousand two hundred thirty-seven **2.** a) three hundred sixty-five b) thirty, thirty-one c) sixty d) three thousand six hundred e) eighty-six thousand four hundred

Number Round Up Page 24

1. 8930, 8900, 9000 **2.** 1100, 1100, 1000 **3.** 7940, 7900, 8000 **4.** 6900, 6900, 7000 **5.** 4650, 4700, 5000 **6.** 8730, 8700, 9000 **7.** 5590, 5600, 6000 **8.** 6740, 6700, 7000 **9.** 5080, 5100, 5000 **10.** 6040, 6000, 6000

Estimating Sums and Differences Page 25

1. a) 20 + 20, 40 b) 40 + 30, 70 c) 50 – 20, 30 d) 80 – 20, 60 **2.** a) 200 + 200, 400 b) 400 – 100, 300 c) 500 + 400, 900 **3.** a) 2000 + 2000, 4000 b) 4000 – 2000, 2000 c) 4000 – 1000, 3000

Add by Making an Easier Problem Page 26

1. a) 18 + 2 = 20, add 20 to 44 to get 64, subtract 2 to get 62, 62 b) 27 + 3 = 30, add 30 to 53 to get 83, subtract 3 to get 80, 53 + 27 = 80 c) 16 + 4 = 20, add 20 to 77 to get 97, subtract 4 to get 93, 77 + 16 = 93 d) 35 + 5 = 40, add 40 to 36 to get 76, subtract 5 to get 71, 36 + 35 = 71 e) 28 + 2 = 30, 63 + 30 = 93, 93 – 2 = 91, 63 + 28 = 91 f) 39 + 1 = 40, 48 + 40 = 88, 88 – 1 = 87, 48 + 39 = 87

2. a) 18 + 2 = 20, 20 + 46 = 66, 66 – 2 = 64, 46 + 18 = 64 b) 16 + 4 = 20, 20 + 59 = 79, 79 – 4 = 75, 59 + 16 = 75 c) 43 + 7 = 50, 50 + 37 = 87, 87 – 7 = 80, 37 + 43 = 80 d) 29 + 1 = 30, 30 + 68 = 98, 98 – 1 = 97, 68 + 29 = 97 e) 35 + 5 = 40, 40 + 26 = 66, 66 – 5 = 61, 26 + 35 = 61 f) 67 + 3 = 70, 70 + 16 = 86, 86 – 3 = 83, 16 + 67 = 83 g) 58 + 2 = 60, 60 + 23 = 83, 83 - 2 = 81, 23 + 58 = 81 h) 26 + 4 = 30, 30 + 71 = 101, 101 - 4 = 97, 26 + 71 = 97

Three-Digit Addition Without Regrouping Page 28

1. First Row: 889, 277, 497, 876, 754 **Second Row:** 948, 898, 795, 785, 959 **Third Row:** 955, 837, 774, 888, 844 **Fourth Row:** 797, 937, 744, 383, 659 **2. First Row:** 167, 886, 737, 677, 486 **Second Row:** 377, 547, 585, 659, 558 **Third Row:** 788, 579, 877, 846, 853 **Fourth Row:** 774, 477, 995, 749, 866 **Fifth Row:** 749, 949, 945, 969, 998

Three-Digit Addition with Regrouping Page 30

1. First Row: 939, 814, 648, 828, 316 **Second Row:** 506, 828, 864, 801, 839 **Third Row:** 839, 616, 517, 545, 822

2. First Row: 596, 781, 782, 744 **Second Row:** 673, 951, 562, 791, 686 **Third Row:** 876, 877, 862, 690, 882

3. 427, 634, 842, 814

Four-Digit Addition with Regrouping Page 32

First Row: 4819, 9690, 9947, 7089, 7297 **Second Row:** 9350, 8790, 6265, 3609, 5809

Third Row: 7129, 7913, 8063, 9191, 8409

Subtract by Making and Easier Problem Page 33

1. a) 29 + 1 = 30, subtract 30 from 34 to get 4, add 1 to get 5, 34 – 29 = 5 b) 27 + 3 = 30, 54 – 30 = 24, 24 + 3 = 27, 54 – 27 = 27 c) 38 +2 = 40, 67 – 40 = 27, 27 + 2 = 29, 67 – 38 = 29 d) 26 + 4 = 30, 71 – 30 = 41, 41 + 4 = 45, 71 – 26 = 45 e) 38 + 2 = 40, 81 – 40 = 41, 41 + 2 = 43, 81 – 38 = 43 f) 47 + 3 = 50, 92 – 50 = 42, 42 + 3 = 45, 92 – 47 = 45

2. a) 29 b) 39 c) 19 d) 39 e) 29 f) 28 g) 26 h) 27

Add and Subtract by Making an Easier Problem Page 35

1. a) 64 b) 75 c) 80 d) 97 e) 61 f) 83 **2.** a) 33 b) 39 c) 19 d) 39 e) 29 f) 28 **3.** a) 277 b) 566 c) 418 d) 629

Taking Apart to Make Tens for Subtraction Page 36

1. a) 16 – 10 = 6 b) 13 + 3 – 7 + 3 = 16 – 10 = 6, 3 c) 17 + 2 – 8 + 2 = 19 – 10 = 9, 2 d) 18 + 1 – 9 + 1 = 19 – 10 = 9, 1 e) 43 + 4 – 6 + 4 = 47 – 10 = 37, 4 f) 34 + 5 – 5 + 5 = 39 – 10 = 29, 5 g) 26 + 3 – 7 + 3 = 29 – 10 = 19, 3

2. a) 34 + 3 – 17 + 3 = 37 – 20 = 17, 3 b) 28 + 1 – 19 + 1 = 29 – 20 = 9, 1 c) 22 + 4 – 16 + 4 = 26 – 20 = 6, 4 d) 34 + 5 – 15 + 5 = 39 – 20 = 19, 5 e) 43 + 5 – 35 + 5 = 48 – 40 = 8, 5 f) 51 + 1 – 39 + 1 = 52 – 40 = 12, 1 g) 35 + 4 – 26 + 4 = 39 – 30 = 9, 4

Math Riddle Page 38

A = 40, C = 36, D = 48, E = 42, F = 81, G = 72, H = 35, I = 20, L = 18, N = 63, O = 70, R = 45, S = 56, T = 100, U = 90, W = 25, Y = 27; He wanted to see a flying saucer!

Three-Digit Subtraction Without Regrouping Page 39

1. First Row: 548, 334, 414, 343, 531 **Second Row:** 555, 554, 203, 131, 441 **Third Row:** 752, 227, 122, 110, 3 **Fourth Row:** 451, 101, 20, 151, 311 **2. First Row:** 12, 615, 144, 23, 165 **Second Row:** 837, 255, 615, 233, 412 **Third Row:** 113, 211, 105, 136, 425 **Fourth Row:** 245, 44, 444, 353, 653

Brain Stretch 1983

Three-Digit Subtraction with Regrouping Page 41

1. First Row: 281, 282, 472, 573, 292 **Second Row:** 270, 380, 143, 251, 174 **Third Row:** 482, 593, 270, 494, 461

2. First Row: 295, 227, 217, 713 **Second Row:** 325, 422, 406, 118, 251 **Third Row:** 749, 214, 37, 156, 238

3. 245, 264, 427, 193, 346

Four-Digit Subtraction with Regrouping Page 43

First Row: 1911, 3181, 1371, 1263, 1412 **Second Row:** 2080, 2205, 1900, 1911, 4239

Third Row: 2517, 1493, 2460, 1591, 3817

Subtraction Match Page 44

Answers to left hand column: 214, 8346, 1396, 3815, 1353, 903, 6731, 4644

Word Problems Page 45

1. a) 405 b) 734 **2.** a) Mr. Kerem's class b) $123 **3.** a) 294 b) 532 **4.** a) 3925 b) 2596

Money Riddle Page 46

A = $1.00, C = $2.35, E = $2.00, G = 75¢, H = $3.00, I = 25¢, N = $2.50, R = $1.20, S = $1.50, T = 50¢, W = $1.25, Y = $4.00; When there is change in the weather.

Counting with Bills and Coins Page 47

2. [image of one twenty dollar bill, one five dollar bill, three quarters (25¢ each) and one dime (10¢)] **3.** [image of one ten dollar bill] **4.** [image of one ten dollar bill, one 5 dollar bill, one toonie ($2), two quarters (25¢ each) and one nickel (5¢)] **5.** [image of one ten dollar bill, one five dollar bill, one loonie ($1) and two dimes (10¢ each)]

Comparing Money Values Page 48

1. a) $8.00 > $7.65 b) $8.35 > $7.30 c) $7.15 < $8.15

Patterns on a 100 Chart Page 49

1. [image of 100 chart with multiples of 3 shaded blue, multiples of four shaded green, multiples of six circled, and multiples of eight squared] **2.** a) When counting by 3s, the ones digit cycles through the following pattern: 3, 6, 9, 2, 5, 8, 1, 4, 7, 0. b) When counting by 6s the ones digit cycles through the following pattern: 6, 2, 8, 4, 0. c) When counting by 4s the ones digit cycles through the following pattern: 4, 8, 2, 6, 0. d) When counting by 8s, the ones digit cycles through the following pattern: 8, 6, 4, 2, 0. **3.** a) The blue shaded numbers form diagonals that run lower left to upper right. Horizontally the numbers have two non-blue squares between them. Vertically, the squares have two non-blue squares between them. b) Green shaded numbers are four away from each other on the diagonal. They are two squares away from each other vertically, and four squares away from each other horizontally.

Arrays Page 50

1. a) 4, 6, 4 × 6 = 24 b) 3, 5, 3 × 5 = 15 c) 3, 3, 3 × 3 = 9 **2.** a) 3 × 7 = 21 b) 6 × 2 = 12 c) 4 × 5 = 20 d) 4 × 3 = 12 e) 2 × 5 = 10 f) 5 × 3 = 15 **3.** a) [image of an array with five rows of four blocks], 5 × 4 = 20 b) [image of an array with four rows of eight blocks], 4 × 8 = 32 c) [image of an array with one row of six blocks], 1 × 6 = 6 d) [image of an array with two rows of nine blocks], 2 × 9 = 18 e) [image of an array with four rows of four blocks], 4 × 4 = 16 f) [image of an array with six rows of three blocks], 6 × 3 = 18 g) [image of an array with six rows of six blocks], 6 × 6 = 36 h) [image of an array with seven rows of one block], 7 × 1 = 7 i) [image of an array with three rows of two blocks], 3 × 2 = 6 j) [image of an array with seven rows of four blocks], 7 × 4 = 28 k) [image of an array with two rows of ten blocks], 2 × 10 = 20 l) [image of an array with three rows of five blocks], 3 × 5 = 15

Using Doubles to Multiply Page 52

1. a) 14, 28 b) 16, 32 c) 10, 20 d) 18, 36 e) 15, 30 f) 18, 36 **2.** a) 55¢ × 2 = 110¢ = $1.10 b) 2 × 80¢ = 160¢, so 4 × 80¢ = 320¢ = $3.20 c) 4 × 12 ¢ = 48¢, so 8 × 12¢ = 96¢ **3.** a) 16, 32, 64 b) 14, 28, 56 **4.** Molly's strategy does work. How students explain will vary. **5.** a) 9, 18, 36 b) 24, 48, 96

Brain Stretch a) 2 × 3 = 6, 4 × 3 = 12, 8 × 3 = 24, 16 × 3 = 48 b) 2 × 5 = 10, 4 × 5 = 20, 8 × 5 = 40, 16 × 5 = 80

Multiply by Adding a Group Page 54

1. 12 + 6 = 18 **2.** 4 × 4 + 4 = 16 + 4 = 20 **3.** 5 × 5 + 5 = 25 + 5 = 30 **4.** 4 × 7 + 7 = 28 + 7 = 35 **5.** 6 × 6 + 6 = 36 + 6 = 42 **6.** 9 × 3 + 9 = 27 + 9 = 36

Multiplying by 4, 5, and 6 Page 55

First Row: 36, 8, 30, 12, 15 **Second Row:** 35, 20, 6, 0, 24 **Third Row:** 20, 18, 40, 4, 24 **Fourth Row:** 0, 54, 10, 36, 25
Brain Stretch 8 × 7 = 56, There were 56 pictures in the photo album.

Using Patterns to Multiply by 9 Page 56

1. a) 9 × 3 = 30 – 3, so 9 × 3 = 27 b) 9 × 7 = 70 – 7, so 9 × 7 = 63 **2.** a) 36, 45, 54, 63, 72, 81, 90 b) The ones digit decreases by one each time, and the tens digit increases by one each time. For each product, the ones and tens digits add together to make a sum of nine.

Multiplying by 7, 8, and 9 Page 57

First Row: 81, 9, 28, 14, 40 **Second Row:** 32, 18, 7, 24, 54 **Third Row:** 64, 21, 0, 45, 63 **Fourth Row:** 0, 49, 16, 35, 42
Brain Stretch Bill is correct. Student explanations may vary.

Match-Up Fun Page 58

Left hand column: 42, 56, 49, 72, 24, 54, 48, 24, 45, 35, 72, 42, 63, 30, 40
Right Hand Column: 24, 54, 48, 45, 42, 63, 40, 49, 72, 42, 56, 30, 72, 24, 35

Multiplication Fact Fun Page 59

1. 2 **2.** 18 **3.** 35 **4.** 54 **5.** 0 **6.** 48 **7.** 16 **8.** 42 **9.** 16 **10.** 18 **11.** 21 **12.** 5 **13.** 0 **14.** 27 **15.** 64 **16.** 28 **17.** 8 **18.** 48 **19.** 81 **20.** 14 **21.** 30 **22.** 36 **23.** 16 **24.** 35 **25.** 0 **26.** 9 **27.** 4 **28.** 9 **29.** 10 **30.** 0 **31.** 36 **32.** 32 **33.** 45 **34.** 27 **35.** 5 **36.** 40 **37.** 49 **38.** 24
1. 16 **2.** 27 **3.** 50 **4.** 0 **5.** 12 **6.** 21 **7.** 24 **8.** 42 **9.** 6 **10.** 36 **11.** 66 **12.** 15 **13.** 25 **14.** 20 **15.** 72 **16.** 4 **17.** 28 **18.** 14 **19.** 18 **20.** 63 **21.** 56 **22.** 9 **23.** 14 **24.** 24 **25.** 12 **26.** 63 **27.** 54 **28.** 40 **29.** 12 **30.** 15 **31.** 30 **32.** 6 **33.** 0 **34.** 24 **35.** 2 **36.** 54 **37.** 7 **38.** 56

Multiply Numbers by Tens Page 61

1. a) [image of two groups of 4 ten blocks], 80 b) [image of 3 groups of two ten blocks], 60 **2.** a) 5, 50 b) 12, 120 c) 21, 210

Multiply Numbers by Hundreds Page 62

1. a) [image of 3 groups of 3 hundred blocks], 900 b) [image of 4 groups of 2 hundred blocks], 800 **2.** a) 24, 240, 2400 b) 40, 400, 4000 c) 36, 360, 3600

Multiply Numbers by Thousands Page 63

1. a) [image of 2 groups of 2 thousand blocks], 4000 b) [image of 3 groups of 3 thousand blocks], 9000 c) [image of 5 groups of 1 thousand blocks], 5000 d) [image of 3 groups of 4 thousand blocks], 12000

Multiply Multiples of 10, 100, and 1000 Page 64

1. a) 12, 120, 1200, 12000 b) 28, 280, 2800, 28000 c) 9, 90, 900, 9000 d) 30, 300, 3000, 30000 e) 16, 160, 1600, 16000 f) 36, 360, 3600, 36000 g) 14, 140, 1400, 14000 h) 15, 150, 1500, 15000 i) 42, 420, 4200, 42000 **2.** a) 6, 60, 600, 6000 b) 4, 40, 400, 4000 c) 8, 80, 800, 8000 **3.** a) 100 b) 1200 c) 4000 d) 1000 e) 240 f) 2100 g) 1800 h) 300 i) 4000

Multiply Two-Digit Numbers by One-Digit Numbers Page 66

1. 74 **2.** 56 **3.** 410 **4.** 146 **5.** 75 **6.** 105 **7.** 228 **8.** 138 **9.** 57 **10.** 52 **11.** 215 **12.** 328 **13.** 30 **14.** 208 **15.** 205 **16.** 46 **17.** 376 **18.** 130 **19.** 134 **20.** 252 **21.** 194 **22.** 126 **23.** 235 **24.** 144 **25.** 272 **26.** 203 **27.** 348 **28.** 228 **29.** 216 **30.** 124 **31.** 450 **32.** 264 **33.** 96 **34.** 192 **35.** 138 **36.** 420 **37.** 352 **38.** 330 **39.** 74 **40.** 182 **41.** 370 **42.** 140 **43.** 165 **44.** 132
Brain Stretch 6km per day × 189 days per year = 1134km per year. Katie walks 1134 km back and forth to school in one year.

Multiply Multi-Digit Numbers Page 69

1. 711 **2.** 628 **3.** 910 **4.** 1492 **5.** 1075 **6.** 405 **7.** 1028 **8.** 2076 **9.** 1914 **10.** 1578 **11.** 1772 **12.** 1410 **13.** 230 **14.** 1300 **15.** 2055 **16.** 699 **17.** 8226 **18.** 2630 **19.** 5016 **20.** 4944 **21.** 4694 **22.** 3654 **23.** 14055 **24.** 12648 **25.** 17072 **26.**10661 **27.** 14106 **28.** 20580

Estimate a Product Page 71

1. a) round 59 to 60, 3 × 60 = 180 b) round 48 to 50, 11 × 50 = 550 c) round 415 to 400, 6 × 400 = 2400 d) round 99 to 100, 6 x 100 = 600 e) round 35 to 40, 8 x 40 = 320 f) round 79 to 80, 50 x 80 = 4000 g) round 18 to 20, 9 × 20 = 180 h) round 49 to 50, 60 × 50 = 300 i) round 94 to 90, 40 × 90 = 3600

2. a) round 25 to 30 and 32 to 30, 30 × 30 = 90 b) round 37 to 40 and 59 to 60, 40 × 60 = 2400 c) round 43 to 40 and 78 to 80, 40 × 80 = 3200 d) round 51 to 50 and 49 to 50, 50 × 50 = 2500 e) round 68 to 70 and 41 to 40, 70 × 40 = 2800 f) round 73 to 70 and 28 to 30, 70 × 30 = 2100 g) round 53 to 50 and 635 to 600, 50 × 600 = 30000 h) round 28 to 30 and 229 to 200, 30 × 200 = 6000 i) round 46 to 50 and 482 to 500, 50 × 500 = 25000

Brain Stretch a) Round 48 to 50 and 287 to 300. 50 × 6 = 300, An estimate of 6 buses will be needed. b) 48 × 6 = 288, which is one more than the required 287. 6 buses will be needed.

Relating Addition and Division Page 73

1. 24, 4 groups of 6, 24 **2.** 35, 7 groups of 5, 35 **3.** 63, 7 groups of 9, 63 **4.** , 30, 3 groups of 10, 10 **5.** 28, 4 groups of 7, 28 **6.** 54, 6 groups of 9, 9 **7.** 72, 9 groups of 8, 72 **8.** 42, 6 groups of 7, 42 **9.** 48, 6 groups of 8, 48 **10.** 54, 9 groups of 6, 6

Related Facts Page 74

First Row: 5, 9, 8 **Second Row:** 3, 7, 8 **Third Row:** 6, 9, 9 **Fourth Row:** 9, 49, 7 **Fifth Row:** 8, 9 **Sixth Row:** 81, 64

Related Facts Continued Page 72

First Row: 2, 5, 4 **Second Row:** 4, 5, 3 **Third Row:** 6, 5, 10 **Fourth Row:** 8, 1, 8 **Fifth Row:** 42, 6 **Sixth Row:** 10, 10

Related Facts Continued Page 73

First Row: 4, 3, 9 **Second Row:** 8, 7, 7 **Third Row:** 8, 3, 63 **Fourth Row:** 8, 8, 21 **Fifth Row:** 7, 9 **Sixth Row:** 4, 90

Using Halving to Divide Page 77

1. a) 12, 6, 6 b) 18, 9, 9 c) 20, 10, 10 d) 24, 12, 12 **2.** a) 8, 4, 2, 2 b) 16, 8, 4, 4 c) 32, 16, 8, 8 d) 24, 12, 6, 6

Brain Stretch 40 ÷ 2 = 20, 20 ÷ 2 = 10, 10 ÷ 2 = 5. So 40 ÷ 8 = 5

Dividing by 4, 5, and 6 Page 79

First Row: 6, 1, 3, 11 **Second Row:** 10, 5, 2, 5 **Third Row:** 7, 7, 1, 11 **Fourth Row:** 7, 4, 11, 3

Dividing by 7, 8, and 9 Page 80

First Row: 7, 12, 3, 2 **Second Row:** 8, 11, 8, 5 **Third Row:** 9, 7, 10,10 **Fourth Row:** 6, 6, 6, 3

Division Fact Fun Page 81

1. 8 **2.** 9 **3.** 3 **4.** 10 **5.** 10 **6.** 18 **7.** 6 **8.** 3 **9.** 8 **10.** 5 **11.** 5 **12.** 5 **13.** 9 **14.** 4 **15.** 8 **16.** 2 **17.** 4 **18.** 3 **19.** 8 **20.** 3 **21.** 9 **22.** 5 **23.** 2 **24.** 10 **25.** 3 **26.** 2 **27.** 8 **28.** 4 **29.** 7 **30.** 10 **31.** 3 **32.** 6 **33.** 6 **34.** 9 **35.** 7 **36.** 7 **37.** 2 **38.** 9 **39.** 10 **40.** 3 **41.** 9 **42.** 7 **43.** 5 **44.** 9 **45.** 2 **46.** 8 **47.** 9 **48.** 1 **49.** 6 **50.** 9 **51.** 10 **52.** 3 **53.** 7 **54.** 8 **55.** 8 **56.** 10 **57.** 2 **58.** 5 **59.** 6 **60.** 3 **61.** 2 **62.** 12 **63.** 2 **64.** 2 **65.** 9 **66.** 1 **67.** 5 **68.** 9 **69.** 5 **70.** 2 **71.** 1 **72.** 1 **73.** 6 **74.** 7 **75.** 7 **76.** 10

Divide Using Blocks Page 83

1. a) 3, 2 tens and 5 ones b) 4, 1 ten and 3 ones **2.** a) 5, 1 ten and 2 ones, 3 leftover b) 4, 1 ten and 8 ones, 2 leftover c) 3, 2 tens and 8 ones, 1 leftover d) 2, 2 tens and 6 ones, 1 leftover e) 4, 2 tens and 4 ones, 2 leftover f) 6, 1 ten and 2 ones, 4 leftover **3.** 88 ÷ 4 = 22, There are 22 trees in each row. Students may use more than one method to solve this problem.

Divide a Two-Digit Number by One-Digit Numbers Page 85

1. 17 R 2 **2.** 27 **3.** 17 R 1 **4.** 28 R 2 **5.** 23 **6.** 24 **7.** 39 R 1 **8.** 16 R 2 **9.** 24 R 2 **10.** 14 R 4 **11.** 14 R 5 **12.** 14 **13.** 10 R 4 **14.** 12 R 4 **15.** 12 R 5 **16.** 22 R 2 **17.** 14 **18.** 12 R 2 **19.** 11 **20.** 14 R 2 **21.** 12 R 1 **22.** 11 R 1 **23.** 12 R 3 **24.** 14 R 3

Divide Multi-Digit Numbers Page 87

1. 271 R 1 **2.** 133 R 3 **3.** 272 **4.** 64 **5.** 178 **6.** 189 R 1 **7.** 135 R 2 **8.** 183 R 3 **9.** 93 R 2 **10.** 124 R 2 **11.** 141

Estimate a Quotient Page 88

1. a) 25 ÷ 5 = 5, estimated quotient is 50 b) 24 ÷ 6 = 4, estimated quotient is 40 c) 32 ÷ 4 = 8, estimated quotient is 80 d) 49 ÷ 7 = 7, estimated quotient is 70 e) 42 ÷ 6 = 7, estimated quotient is 70 f) 12 ÷ 3 = 4, estimated quotient is 40
2. a) 15 ÷ 3 = 5, estimated quotient is 50 b) 24 ÷ 4 = 6, estimated quotient is 60 c) 20 ÷ 5 = 4, estimated quotient is 40 d) 35 ÷ 5 = 7, estimated quotient is 70 e) 42 ÷ 6 = 7, estimated quotient is 70 f) 64 ÷ 8 = 8, estimated quotient is 80

Word Problems Page 90

1. Divide, 33 students were in each bus **2.** Multiply, She biked 288km in total. **3.** Divide, There will be five tickets left over. **4.** Multiply, Each Canadian uses 2303 litres of water in a week.

Add Decimal Numbers Page 91

1. a) 7.4 b) 5.1 c) 6.5 d) 6.3

Subtract Decimal Numbers Page 93

1. a) 1.4 b) 1.5 c) 1.8 d) 0.9

Comparing Fractions Page 95

1. ¼ < ½ **2.** 1/9 > 1/10 **3.** 1/9 < 1/4 **4.** 1/7 > 1/10 **5.** 1/8 < 1/2 **6.** 6/7 > 6/8 **7.** ½ >1/5 **8.** 1/8 < 1/7 **9.** 1/3 >1/9 **10.** ½ < 6/8

Equivalent Fractions Page 96

1. 8/10 = 4/5 **2.** ½ = 3/6 **3.** 1/3 = 2/6 **4.** 2/10 = 1/5 **5.** 2/8 = 1/4 **6.** ½ = 5/10 **7.** 2/10 = 1/5 **8.** 1/3 = 3/9

Adding Fractions Page 97

2. 2/2 = 1 **3.** 6/9 = 2/3 **4.** 7/7 = 1 **5.** 6/6 = 1 **6.** 4/5 **7.** 2/3 **8.** 8/8 = 1 **9.** 6/8 = 3/4 **10.** ¾ **11.** 9/9 = 1 **12.** 4/5 **13.** 3/7 **14.** 3/3 = 1 **15.** 6/6 = 1

Brain Stretch The circle depicting ¼ should be circled.

Subtracting Fractions Page 98

2. 1/4 **3.** 1/3 **4.** 5/7 **5.** 2/4 = 1/2 **6.** 3/5 **7.** 1/6 **8.** 2/9 **9.** 2/7 **10.** 1/8 **11.** 1/9 **12.** 2/5 **13.** 7/9 **14.** 2/6 = 1/3 **15.** 4/7

Brain Stretch 5 creatures are left.

Exploring Decimal Fractions Page 99

First Row: 0.08, 0.6, 0.05 **Second Row:** 0.9, 0.8, 0.76 **Third Row:** 0.17, 0.5, 0.1

What Time is It? Page 100

1. 9:22 **2.** 3:37 **3.** 5:33 **4.** 10:47 **5.** 8:12 **6.** 12:32

Draw the Hands Page 101

1. [image of clock showing 10:36] **2.** [image of clock showing 5:07] **3.** [image of clock showing 5:42] **4.** [image of clock showing 3:21] **5.** [image of clock showing 1:16] **6.** [image of clock showing 6:28] **7.** [image of clock showing 2:03] **8.** [image of clock showing 3:51]

Elapsed Time Page 102

1. 3:40, 5:35, 1 hour, 55 minutes **2.** 12:30, 1:25, 55 minutes **3.** 4:15, 6:10, 1 hour, 55 minutes

Basketball Fun Page 103

1. Sunday: 6:10, Monday: 5:55, Tuesday: 6:00, Wednesday: 7:00, Thursday: 6:05, Friday: 4:30, Saturday: 5:30

2. 175 minutes, or 2 hours and 55 minutes.

Brain Stretch a) 7:40am b) 2:55pm

Solve Problems About Time Page 104

1. a) Estimates may vary. b) She will get to school at 8:25. **2.** Answers will vary. **3.** a) 2:55 b) 4:50 c) 6:25 d) 6:59 **4.** 3:45 **5.** a) 1:60, 2:00 b) 6:65, 7:05 c) 11:85, 12:25 d) 11:75, 12:15 **6.** Adam stopped playing at 6:00.

Week 1

Mon. **1.** 14 **2.** 7 **3.** 15, 18, 21 **4.** shrinking **5.** 10, 15, 20, 25

Tues. **1.** 6 **2.** 7911, 7918, 8791 **3.** 6531 **4.** 460, 280 **5.** 15

Wed. **1.** trapezoid or quadrilateral **2.** 3 or more **3.** cone **4.** turn
5. a 4 sided figure/polygon

Thurs. **1.** 10mm **2.** 4:45 **3.** cm **4.** kilometre **5.** 18, 16

Fri. **1.** 42 **2.** hockey **3.** 2 **4.** soccer, basketball, hockey **5.** ans. will vary

Brain Stretch 52, 104, 260

Week 2

Mon. **1.** 15 **2.** 25, 30, 35 **3.** 11, 22, 11 **4.** 40, 30, 20 **5.** 9

Tues. **1.** 12 205 **2.** 4723, 7324, 7432 **3.** 6541 **4.** 1300, 2700 **5.** $28.55

Wed. **1.** pentagon **2.** 2 sets/pairs **3.** cylinder **4.** flip **5.** ans. vary

Thurs. **1.** 1000 **2.** a **3.** a **4.** 3:35 **5.** m

Fri. **1.** reggae 卌 卌 II classical II dance 卌 卌 卌 卌 卌 III rock 卌 卌 卌 II
country 卌 卌 IIII **2.** dance music **3.** classical **4.** 14 **5.** 73

Brain Stretch 634

Week 3

Mon. **1.** 25 **2.** growing **3.** 22 **4.** 8 **5.** 55, 66, 77

Tues. **1.** 8983 **2.** 5 **3.** 650 **4.** 816 **5.** $26.25

Wed. **1.** right triangle **2.** 2 sets/pairs **3.** square prism or cube **4.** a **5.** 8, 8

Thurs. **1.** 100 **2.** 20 **3.** m or km **4.** 1:40 **5.** 10

Fri. **1.** title- answers will vary X-axis number of votes **2.** blue **3.** green, yellow **4.** 36

Brain Stretch ans. will vary

Week 4

Mon. **1.** growing **2.** growing and repeating **3.** decreasing **4.** 35 **5.** 11

Tues. **1.** 2543, 2745, 3245 **2.** 5028, 5208, 8052 **3.** 3353 **4.** 180 **5.** 8621

Wed. **1.** parallelogram or quadrilateral **2.** octagon **3.** 0 **4.** 3 **5.** square based pyramid

Thurs. **1.** 60 **2.** 7 **3.** mm or cm **4.** 8:30 am **5.** 16 cm, 12 cm^2

Fri. **1.** Oak Town **2.** Birch Town **3.** 80 **4.** 60 mm **5.** Birch, Pine, Maple,
Spruce, Elm, Oak

Brain Stretch 14 m = 1400 cm

Week 5

Mon. **1.** 2, 4, 6, 8 **2.** 1, 6, 11, 16 **3.** 20, 18, 16, 14 **4.** 3, 6, 9, 12 **5.** 8

Tues. **1.** 9419 **2.** 5280 **3.** 5821 **4.** = **5.** 7431

Wed. **1.** octagon **2.** pentagon **3.** 1 **4.** 5 **5.** cube or square prism

Thurs. **1.** 30 **2.** 48 m **3.** 9 **4.** 9:55 **5.** 50 m

Fri. cars – 11 trucks – 4 vans – 13 buses – 22 **1.** 50 **2.** buses **3.** 2 **4.** 18 **5.** 18

Brain Stretch 3 computers

Week 6

Mon. **1.** 30, 35, 40, 45 **2.** 100, 80, 60, 40 **3.** 9 **4.** start at 8, multiply by 2 **5.** 7

Tues. **1.** (200+ 100=300) ans. may vary **2.** 900 +500=1400 (ans. may vary) **3.** 479 **4.**787 **5.** 381

Wed. **1.** a point where 2 sides of a figure meet **2.** 4 **3.** 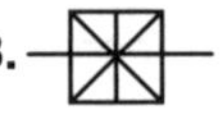 **4.** sphere **5.** 

Thurs. **1.** ans. will vary –3 by 8, 4 by 6 **2.** 28 units^2 **3.** ans. will vary – 1 by 5, 2 by 4, 3 by 3 **4.** 8:55 **5.** 240 mins

Fri. **1.** cats **2.** 75 **3.** 14 **4.** 25

Brain Stretch 3.5h per week 15 hrs. per month (based on a 30 day month)

Week 7

Mon. **1.** 7 **2.** 1 **3.** 30 **4.** 68 **5.** ans. will vary

Tues. **1.** 80 **2.** 200 **3.** 114 **4.** 121 **5.** $54.00

Wed. **1.**  **2.** 5 sides **3.** no **4.** all except triangle **5.** circle

Thurs. **1.** ans. will vary **2.** 8000 **3.** mL **4.** 3:20 p.m. **5.** 32 cm 63 cm^2

Fri. **1.** not likely **2.** very likely **3.** 3/10 **4.** 7/10 **5.** ans. may vary

Brain Stretch **1.** 50 m **2.** 150 m^2 **3.** $500.00

Week 8

Mon. **1.** 4, 16, 64, 256 **2.** 2, 6, 18, 54 **3.** 49 **4.** start at 99, subtract 11 **5.** ans. will vary

Tues. **1.** 6039 **2.** 1004 **3.** 40 **4.** 19 **5.** 62

Wed. **1.** false **2.** c **3.** 8 **4.** ans. will vary **5.** first pair

Thurs. **1.** 20 cm **2.** 200 000 **3.** c **4.** 300 **5.** 12 units^2

Fri. **1.** 1/6 **2.** 1/6 **3.** 3/6 or ½. 3/6 or ½ **4.** impossible **5.** each tally mark =1, = 34

Brain Stretch **1.** .5 L **2.** 13 jars **3.** $26.00

Week 9

Mon. **1.** 81, 243, 729 **2.** 20, 24, 28 **3.** 24, 30, 36 **4.** 12, 10, 8 **5.** ans. will vary

Tues. **1.** 1, 2, 3, 4, 6, 8, 12, 24 **2.** 2 R3 **3.** 40 000+5000+20+3 **4.** 2512 **5.** 2465

Wed. **1.** b **2.** isosceles **3.** a **4.** acute **5.** cylinder, cone, sphere

Thurs. **1.** 2 **2.** 16000 **3.** 17.2 cm **4.** 30 **5.** 9 m^2

Fri. **1.** circle or pie **2.** amusement park **3.** swim, shop and eat, go to amusement park **4.** sleeping **5.** ans. will vary (Disney World, Florida)

Brain Stretch oldest – Vivienne

Week 10

Mon. **1.** yes **2.** 9 **3.** ans. will vary **4.** a **5.** 90

Tues. **1.** 9 **2.** 9832 **3.** 1048 **4.** 7450, 4879, 4531, 1751 **5.** $47.80

Wed. **1.** 0 **2.** rectangle **3.** 5 **4.** rectangular prism **5.** isosceles, equilateral, scalene, right

Thurs. **1.** 11:10 **2.** 6000 m **3.** 40 units **4.** 1984 **5.** 3

Fri. **1.** all except Josie **2.** Martin, Darcy, Martha, Michael **3.** all **4.** 37

Brain Stretch all together = 5.3 km 0 .7 km farther

Week 11

Mon. **1.** 34, 44, 54 **2.** 160, 320, 640 **3.** 72 **4.** 150 **5.** ans. will vary

Tues. **1.** 7/8, 4/8, 2/8 **2.** 3/5, 2/5, 1/5 **3.** 2/7 **4.** 4 **5.** 3 loonies, 2 dimes

Wed. **1.** 2 **2.** hexagon **3.** parallelogram, square, rectangle **4.** none **5.** 1

Thurs. **1.** 11:45 **2.** 3:10 pm **3.** 26 cm **4.** 1944 **5.** a- 4 mins

Fri. **1.** 170 **2.** snowboarding **3.** ice fishing **4.** 40 **5.** 90

Brain Stretch each day = 71 in a week = 497

Week 12

Mon. **1.** ans. will vary **2.** 4 **3.** 55, 66, 77 **4.** 12, 28 **5.** 3

Tues. **1.** 1/5, 3/5, 4/5 **2.** .4 **3.** 57/100 **4.** 3/7 **5.** $67.75

Wed. **1.** obtuse **2.** 0 **3.** 4 **4.** a closed figure with 3 or more sides **5.** AB - CD

Thurs. **1.** 11:40 **2.** 5:00 pm **3.** 18, 16 **4.** 8hrs. 50mins. **5.** 600 000

Fri. ans. will vary for all

Brain Stretch **1.** 99 m **2.** 432 **3.** 4:00 pm

Week 13

Mon. **1.** ans. will vary **2.** 5, 5, 5, 5, 5 **3.** 15 **4.** yes **5.** 44

Tues. **1.** $90.00 **2.** $480.00 **3.** ans. will vary **4.** $35.00 **5.** $18.55

Wed. **1.** 0 **2.** parallel lines **3.** ans. will vary **4.** equilateral **5.** slide

Thurs. **1.** 9 units^2 **2.** 12:45 **3.** check ans. with a ruler **4.** a **5.** 1000

Fri. **1.** 3 **2.** 2 **3.** 5 **4.** 2

Brain Stretch **1.** $130.00 **2.** between 11:00 a.m. and 11:30 a.m. **3.** $4.75

Week 14

Mon. **1.** ans. will vary **2.** 5 **3.** 2 **4.** ice cream **5.** 5x5 or 1x25

Tues. **1.** $5.70 **2.** $11.80 **3.** ans. will vary **4.** ans. will vary **5.** $22.00

Wed. **1.** 4 **2.** 6 **3.** similar **4.** circle **5.** 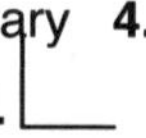

Thurs. **1.** 40 units **2.** 6:05 **3.** 2450 **4.** 5 cm x 5 cm **5.** 40

Fri. **1.** 5/10 or 1/2 **2.** 3/10 **3.** 2/10 or 1/5 **4.** 10/10 **5.** 0/10

Brain Stretch **1.** It's better to buy a dozen because if you bought 12 individually it would cost $7.20. By buying the dozen at $5.95 you will save $1.25. **2.** $1.05

Week 15

Mon. **1.** 3, 6, 12, 24 **2.** 10 **3.** 5, 6, 7 **4.** yes **5.** ans. will vary

Tues. **1.** hundreds **2.** 2342 **3.** 907 **4.** 7 **5.** 476

Wed. **1.** 180 degrees **2.** 2 **3.** ans. will vary depending on the base **4.** ans. will vary **5.** no

Thurs. **1.** .04 **2.** metre stick **3.** c **4.** 3 **5.** 5-10 seconds (will vary)

Fri. **1.** pancakes **2.** grilled cheese **3.** 42 **4.** 10

Brain Stretch **1.** 3.5 kg **2.** 2.8 kg **3.** 123.7 kg

Week 16

Mon. **1.** 2 **2.** 55 **3.** repeating **4.** oval **5.** 3, 4, 4, 1

Tues. **1.** ans. will vary – 2/4, 3/6 **2.** ans. will vary – 6/8 **3.** 2/3 **4.** 3/4 **5.** 3/5

Wed. **1.** true **2.**  **3.** 0 **4.** congruent **5.** 2

Thurs. **1.** measure for accuracy **2.** 8:28 am **3.** 9 cm^2 **4.** 200 **5.** century = 100 yrs, millennium = 1000 years

Fri. **1.** 4 **2.** Friday **3.** 27th **4.** 18th **5.** Friday

Brain Stretch **1.** 155 **2.** 18

Week 17

Mon. **1.** 9 **2.** 14, 17, 20 **3.** no **4.** 7, 11, 15, 19 **5.** 16, 19, 22

Tues. **1.** ans. will vary –4,6,10 **2.** ans. will vary – 1, 3, 5 **3.** 1536 **4.** 152 **5.** 18

Wed. **1.** ans. will vary **2.** ans. will vary **3.** 1 **4.** 25 degrees, scalene **5.** see reflection

Thurs. **1.** 6 **2.** 63 min or 1h 3 min **3.** = **4.** 1 min **5.** 5.4 cm

Fri. **1.** Friday **2.** Monday **3.** 30 **4.** 20

Brain Stretch sphere, cone, cylinder

Week 18

Mon. **1.** ans. will vary **2.** ans. will vary **3.** no **4.** 104, 94, 84 **5.** start at 144, subtract 10

Tues. **1.** 6 **2.** 6.29 **3.** 45 **4.** 70 **5.** 48

Wed. **1.** 6 **2.** similar **3.** 5 **4.** square based pyramid **5.** two shapes the same size and shape

Thurs. **1.** scale **2.** 21.6 cm^2 **3.** a **4.** 200 min **5.** 104

Fri. **1.** basketball **2.** football **3.** 22

Brain Stretch (based on 30 day month) **1.** 26 h **2.** 338 h

Week 19

Mon. **1.** 15 **2.** 35 **3.** 32 **4.** 17, 20, 23, 26, 29 **5.** 9x9 = 81

Tues. **1.** 2360 **2.** 7 **3.** 2.618 **4.** 44 **5.** $62.49

Wed. **1.** acute **2.** right **3.** see picture **4.** ans. will vary **5.** 12

Thurs. **1.** 28 $units^2$ **2.** a **3.** 6 **4.** 1400 m **5.** measure with a ruler for accuracy

Fri. **1.** 9 **2.** 12 **3.** 20 wpm **4.** 11 wpm **5.** 18

Brain Stretch **1.** $9.55 **2.** $3.18, $3.18, $3.19

Week 20

Mon. **1.** no **2.** 245, 250, 255 **3.** 93, 89, 85 **4.** 19 **5.** start at 1000, subtract 100

Tues. **1.** 12 **2.** 8 **3.** 24 **4.** 24 **5.** ans. will vary

Wed. **1.** ans. will vary **2.** 6 **3.** straight angle **4.** 2 **5.** 15 degrees, scalene

Thurs. **1.**  **2.** 96 units **3.** 9:45 pm **4.** 11:00 **5.** 1 h 20 min

Fri. **1.** joke books **2.** science fiction **3.** joke, fiction, comic **4.** 90 **5.** 21

Brain Stretch 8

Week 21

Mon. **1.** 147 **2.** 115 **3.** rectangle **4.** 31, 38, 45 **5.** growing

Tues. **1.** 4 **2.** 9000 **3.** 6/20 **4.** > **5.** $4.00

Wed. **1.** no **2.** ans will vary **3.** 2 **4.** none **5.** a

Thurs. **1.** 22 **2.** measuring cup **3.** 10 000 g **4.** 2.1 **5.** >

Fri. **1.** chocolate **2.** maple walnut **3.** vanilla, bubblegum **4.** 56 **5.** 14

Brain Stretch $66.60

Week 22

Mon. **1.** 8x4 – ans. may vary **2.** no **3.** 9 **4.** start at 900, subtract 50 **5.** growing

Tues. **1.** 7 R1 **2.** 11 R2 **3.** 40 **4.** 54 **5.** 5 groups R2

Wed. **1.** pentagon **2.** square **3.**  e **4.** no **5.** cylinder – 2, 0, 0

Thurs. **1.** L **2.** a **3.** 28 min **4.** 50 **5.** 5:14 pm

Fri. **1.** 3/20 **2.** 2/20 or 1/10 **3.** 5/20 or 1/4 **4.** 12/20 or 3/5 **5.** 0/20

Brain Stretch 2

Week 23

Mon. **1.** 12 **2.** 79, 85, 91 **3.** true **4.** 202, 208, 214, 220 **5.** 48

Tues. **1.** 53 **2.** 31 **3.** 11/30 **4.** 27 **5.** 10

Wed. **1.** obtuse **2.** 2 **3.**  **4.** 0 **5.** b

Thurs. **1.** 3.305 **2.** 1x18, 2x9, or 3x6 **3.** 24 **4.** a **5.** 3 min 20 s

Fri. **1.** d **2.** b **3.** a and c

Brain Stretch $12.00

Week 24

Mon. **1.** 90, 85, 79 **2.** → **3.** yes **4.** start at 99, subtract 6 **5.** 2

Tues. **1.** $29.85 **2.** 7397 **3.** 67 272 **4.** 63 **5.** 5.8

Wed. **1.** 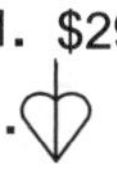 **2.** no **3.** congruent **4.** 1- if it's a right angle triangle **5.** slide or flip

Thurs. **1.** 21 **2.** 11 m **3.** metre stick **4.** 16, 11 **5.** 30 000

Fri. **1.** 23 **2.** 11 **3.** 18 **4.** 28 **5.** 5

Brain Stretch **1.** 72 cards **2.** $6.24

Week 25

Mon. **1.** no **2.** 7 **3.** 37, 45, 53 **4.** 9 **5.** 60, 53, 46, 39, 32

Tues. **1.** 2469 **2.** forty-three dollars and eighty-nine cents **3.** 67/100 **4.** 10.1 **5.** 69

Wed. **1.** 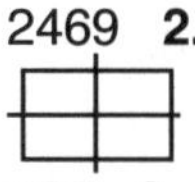 ans. will vary **2.** 4 **3.** i.e 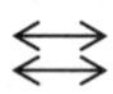 **4.** 10 **5.** c

Thurs. **1.** 730 **2.** 13 units^2 **3.** measure for accuracy **4.**  **5.** all sides will be 6 units

Fri. **1.** 226 **2.** 100 m sprint **3.** high jump **4.** 91 **5.** 46

Brain Stretch 3.9 min

Week 26

Mon. **1.** start at 60, add 15 **2.** no **3.** c **4.** ans. will vary **5.** 55

Tues. **1.** 8 **2.** 3 x toonie, 1 x loonie, 2 x quarter, 2 x dime **3.** .89 **4.** 390 **5.** $7.75

Wed. **1.** 0 **2.** drawing: an angle less than 90° **3.**  **4.** 3 possible, drawn through each vertex

5. **circle** – no angles, no sides, circular lines, no vertices **triangle** – 3 angles, 3 sides, 3 vertices

Thurs. **1.**  **2.** a **3.** February 20th **4.** 600 **5.** 2.680

Fri. **1.** week 1 **2.** $22.00 **3.** $78.00 **4.** $6.00

Brain Stretch **1.** 720 m^2 **2.** 108 m **3.** $864.00

Week 27

Mon. **1.** 220, 209, 198, 187, 176, 165 **2.** 10 **3.** b **4.** start at 2, add 11 **5.** 88, 87, 89

Tues. **1.** 9801, 8901, 8109 **2.**  **3.** 2000 **4.** 2/3 **5.** 7/8

Wed. **1.** 1 **2.** obtuse **3.** 0 **4.**  **5.** triangles

Thurs. **1.** 49 dm^2 **2.** 208 **3.** 6 minutes **4.** ruler **5.** each side is 5 units

Fri. symbol will vary, key = 2

Brain Stretch 80

Week 28

Mon. **1.** 4 **2.** 59, 57, 55 **3.** no **4.** 56 **5.** b

Tues. **1.** 3/6 or 1/2 **2.** 523 **3.** two thousand seven hundred forty five **4.** 48 **5.** 7

Wed. **1.** 4 **2.** see reflection **3.** 0 **4.** 0 **5.** ans. will vary

Thurs. **1.** a **2.** horse **3.** 30 m **4.** 41 **5.** 2190

Fri. **1.** 100 **2.** 20 **3.** 100 **4.** 20 **5.** 80

Brain Stretch **1.** 80 **2.** about 4

Week 29

Mon. **1.** ans. will vary **2.** 200, 185, 170 **3.** a **4.** 15 **5.** 8

Tues. **1.** 0.1289 **2.** 6/10 or 0.6 **3.** 334, 345, 435, 545, **4.** $5.00 **5.** 1, 2, 3, 4, 6, 8, 9, 12, 18, 24, 36, 72

Wed. **1.** false **2.** ans. will vary **3.**  **4.** yes **5.** ans. will vary

Thurs. **1.** 24 mm **2.** 4 **3.** ans. will vary – 9 x 8 **4.** check for accuracy with a ruler **5.** 12 h

Fri. **1.** 600 **2.** comedy **3.** 600 **4.** action and horror **5.** 3450

Brain Stretch 4000 m

Week 30

Mon. **1.** 1728 **2.** no **3.** 16 **4.** start at 32, add 4 **5.** 135 km

Tues. **1.** 1, 2, 3, 4, 6, 8, 12,16, 24, 48 **2.** 6 R2 **3.** 60 000+7000+500+20+3 **4.** 48342 **5.** 9900

Wed. **1.** no **2.** true **3.** 12 **4.**  **5.** 2 figures that have the same size and shape

Thurs. **1.** .11 m **2.**  **3.** 560 min **4.** 8 m^2 **5.** clock

Fri. **1.** spinner 1 **2.** spinner 2 **3.** spinner 1 **4.** d

Brain Stretch **1.** 15 **2.** $45.00 **3.** 45